London's Dock Railways

Part 2:
The Royal Docks, North Woolwich and Silvertown

Dave Marden

©Kestrel Railway Books and Dave Marden 2013

Kestrel Railway Books
PO Box 269
SOUTHAMPTON
SO30 4XR

www.kestrelrailwaybooks.co.uk

All rights reserved.

No part of this publication may be
reproduced, stored in a retrieval system,
transmitted in any form or by any means,
electronic, mechanical, or photocopied,
recorded or otherwise, without the
consent of the publisher in writing.

Printed by the Amadeus Press

ISBN 978-1-905505-28-9

Front cover: A scene that sums up the very nature of the docks and its railways on 25th September 1957 as PLA No 59 (HC No 1245) traverses the quayside at the King George V Dock. A cloth capped port worker passes by on a scooter while another studies his vehicle under the shadow of the Royal Mail cargo ship "Balantia".
(R C Riley / Transport Treasury)

The photographs on the back cover illustrate the final years of the docks railways.

Top: *Dieselisation came to London's Docks in 1959 when many still serviceable steam locomotives were sent to the scrap yard. This line of castoffs was captured on 30th April 1960 and marked the end of an era.*
(R C Riley / Transport Treasury)
Bottom left: *One of the new breed of diesel engines was PLA No 238 (YE No 2763) pictured when new in 1959 at the Royal Docks. This modernisation failed to combat the growing influence of road transport and changes to cargo handling as the dock railways were closed by 1970. (Brian Webb Collection / Industrial Railway Society)*
Bottom right: *Services through the Connaught Tunnel to North Woolwich ceased on 2006 and the line fell into disuse. This desolate scene was photographed in 2010 but the line will be revived as part of the new Crossrail scheme running under the capital linking Abbey Wood to Maidenhead. (Courtesy of Crossrail Ltd)*

Contents

Introduction iv

Part 1 – The Royal Docks
Chapter 1: The Victoria Docks 1
Chapter 2: The Victoria and Albert Docks 3
Chapter 3: The Royal Docks 27
Chapter 4: War and Peace at the Royals 49

Part 2 – Passenger and other Railways
Chapter 5: The Royal Albert Dock Passenger Railway 87
Chapter 6: The North Woolwich Railway 101
Chapter 7: The Silvertown Tramway 113
Chapter 8: Contractors Railways 125

Index 127

Acknowledgements

As with Part 1, my fellow members of both the Industrial Railway Society and the Industrial Locomotive Society have, as always, been most helpful with information from their publications and exhaustive records but, above all, their personal support has been invaluable. Others have given assistance which is greatly appreciated. They are, principally, the Island History Trust, the Museum of London's Docklands, and the London Borough of Tower Hamlets. Once again, the ticket images are from the collection of Michael and Elizabeth Stewart.

I have again made reference to the 1950s articles published by the Industrial Locomotive Society which were compiled by their Librarian, George Groves which, apart from his own recollections, included those of his father Sam who was a driver on PLA locos prior to World War One and had contact with other employees whose memories spanned many earlier decades. Their observations have been a valuable insight into life on the docks railways.

Finally, I must also include the help given by Colin Withey who was at the PLA from 1957 to 1984 and offered me access to his notes from board minutes and also to his collection of photographs acquired during his time there. These were approved with permission of use and are credited accordingly as PLA/Colin Withey Collection. Thanks also to former PLA Librarian Bob Aspinal and PLA Photographer Roy Johnson, and to former PLA loco drivers George Musgrave and Harry Richardson for imparting their recollections of times past.

Where sources of photographs are known they are acknowledged and credited following reasonable attempts to establish reproduction rights and to contact photographers for permission to use them. Any infringement of copyright is unintentional, for which I apologise sincerely.

The following have proved important sources of information:

P.L.A. Railways by Thomas B. Peacock
Industrial Locomotives of the County of London by Robin Waywell and Frank Jux
Industrial Locomotives of Essex by Robin Waywell and Frank Jux
Railway Bylines magazine - various issues and articles by Martin Smith
Disused Stations website by Nick Catford
British History Online website – editor Hermione Hobhouse

Dave Marden 2013

Introduction

This second volume of the book features the dock railways and locomotives at what became known as the Royal Group, primarily the Victoria, Albert and King George V Docks, and also includes other associated and industrial railways in the vicinity. In Part One we saw how the earliest dock companies came into being and evolved into the eventual cramped facilities around the Isle of Dogs, these being The East & West Indias, together with Millwall Docks and other related quays in the locality. They are all covered extensively in that volume, including the railways at Tilbury Docks that were also owned and operated by the East & West India Dock Company.

The act of 1799, permitting the building of the early docks, sought to appease the concerns of the established lightermen, by way of the "Free Water Clause" which entitled them free access to ships in the docks permitting them to transfer cargoes to and from vessels without landing them ashore, and, by transporting the goods to other wharves along the Thames, they avoided the Dock Company's dues. Details of several railway company wharves appear in Part One.

As in Part One it is important to show the how the various docks were administered during their evolution up until the formation of the Port of London Authority in 1909. The following is a summary in respect of the docks that formed the Royal Group.

With the East and West India docks already established along with those at Millwall, the opening of the Royal Albert Docks in 1880 by the London & St Katharine Docks Company (followed by the Tilbury Docks in 1886) had led to an overcapacity of facilities and much cutting of rates which proved disastrous for the industry. Such competition between the Indias and the L&StKD companies brought about severe financial problems, exacerbated by unrest in the workforce when wages were cut and maintenance was reduced.

With the East & West India Dock Company having gone into receivership on the 5th March 1888, the formation of the London & India Docks Joint Committee came about on 1st January 1889 to oversee the running of both companies, who each remained independent under the administration until 1898.

The Joint Committee set up an agreement whereby the two bodies, together with those at the Surrey Commercial and the Millwall Docks, would concur to avoid duplication of services and to harmonise rates and charges. This lead to an improved financial situation which, in turn, allowed for much needed investment. Having succeeded in stabilising the industry, the Joint Committee was able to upgrade much of the obsolete dock equipment and the internal railways, allowing for some modernisation of the rolling stock. The administration ended on the 1st January 1901 with the formation of the London & India Docks Company that had jurisdiction over all docks north of the Thames with the exception of Millwall and Poplar, who maintained their independence from the former two organisations.

The practices and standards brought about by the Joint Committee were maintained and, by 1902, Royal Commission plans were already in place for a single

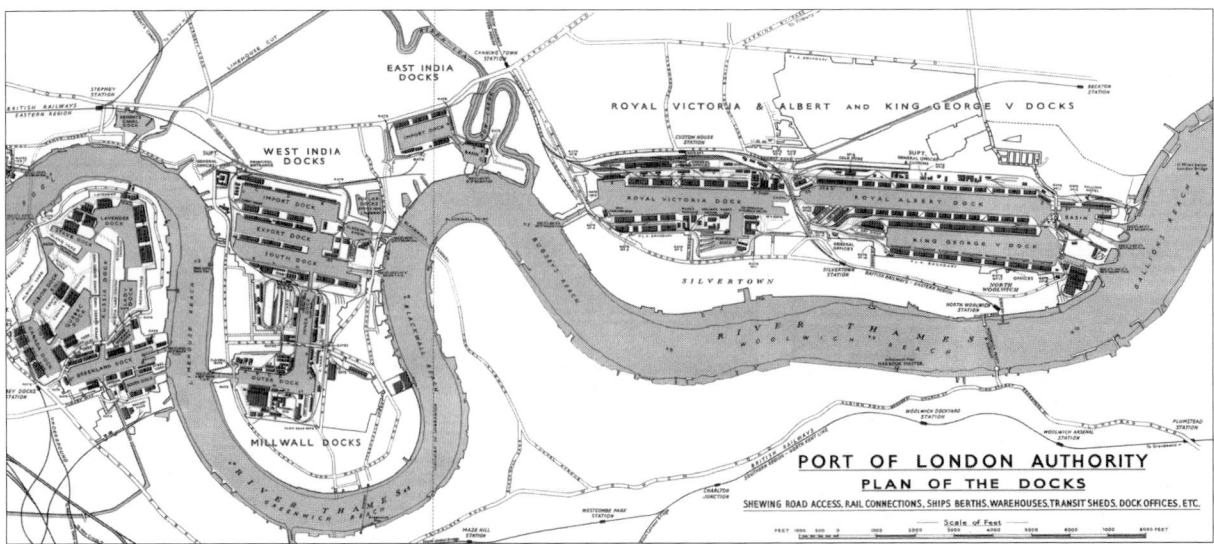

London's principal docks at their peak in 1955 showing the Surrey Commercial Docks on the left beside the West India and Millwall Docks on the Isle of Dogs, and the Royal Docks of Victoria, Albert and King George V on the right. (Author's Collection)

Introduction

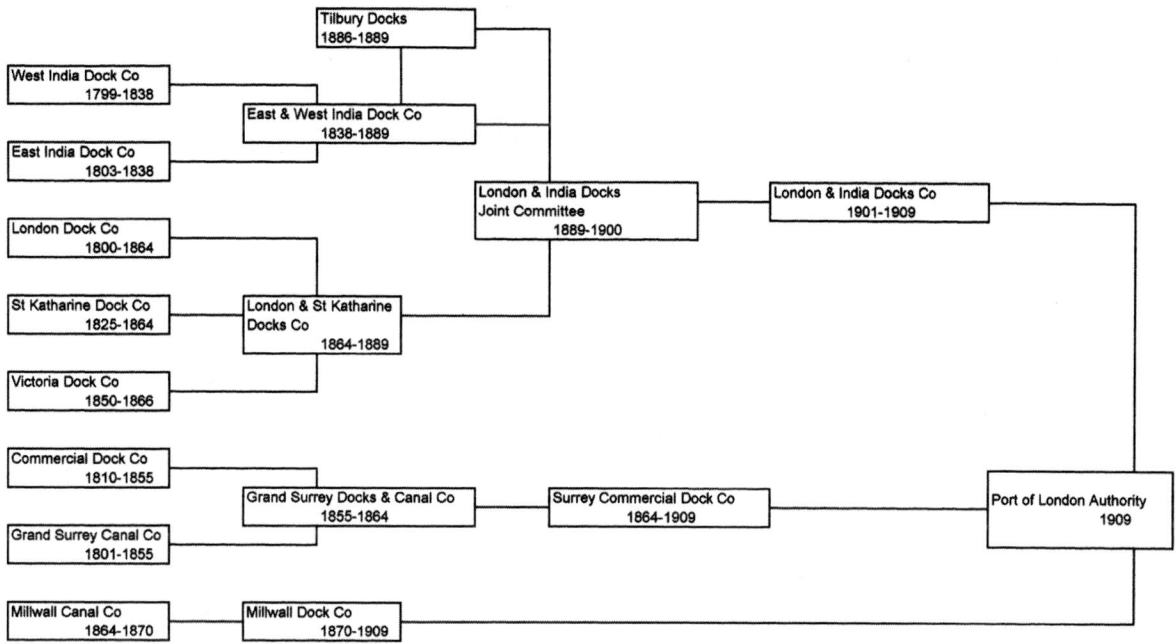

A "Family Tree" of the PLA showing the evolution of the various dock companies until its formation in 1909.

port authority to oversee all aspects of docks and conservancy in the Port of London. This discouraged further investment before a Government bill was passed in 1908 allowing a public body, the Port of London Authority, to take over on 31st March 1909 and, in doing so, absorb the previously independent Millwall Docks. The original eight dock companies were now just one across five major groups, being the London & St Katharine, Surrey Commercial, India & Millwall, Royal, and Tilbury.

In respect of the railways and locomotives contained within the docks systems there now evolved a degree of standardisation where, for operational purposes, the railways were divided into three areas of control. These being at India & Millwall, The Royal Docks, and Tilbury.

To transport, the vast hoards of dock workers, passenger services were also created and, in the case of the Royal Albert Docks Passenger Railway, were also operated by the dock owners. The North Woolwich Railway is also included in this volume due to its close association with the docks and its workers, as is the Silvertown Tramway, a vital industrial railway artery. At the Royal Docks (as with Tilbury), railway company passenger trains were permitted access to the dock lines, subject to a PLA pilot boarding during the visit.

A few facts mentioned in Part One are worth repeating. At its peak the PLA estate covered some 4,203 acres of which 722 were water filled docks that had 45 miles of quays. On taking over such an empire, the new authority had the daunting task of modernising not only the dock infrastructure, but also the many miles of railways contained within them together with numerous swing bridges and signalling networks. Forty one locomotives had been collectively inherited from the various dock companies, with many in a sorry state of repair. The renewal of track and motive power began in earnest in 1911 and continued throughout the following decades until the 1960s, before the eventual closure of the system came in 1970. Over the years, a total of 84 locos were obtained by the PLA, either new or second hand while others came in on loan during busy times or shortages. In total, no less than 112 steam locos worked for the various dock owners until, in the final years of operation, the PLA railway went over to diesel power with many "nearly new" and useful steam locomotives being scrapped in the wake of modernisation.

The initial variety of makers' designs gradually gave way to standardisation and while some early engines were perhaps odd and quirky, the later six-coupled tank engines became synonymous as the "PLA design". In all cases I have used ex-works dates in each

London's Dock Railways: The Royal Docks, North Woolwich and Silvertown

loco history and this may occasionally differ slightly from that on the maker's plate.

Of the three main locomotive depots, Custom House at the Victoria Docks was by far the biggest and busiest. The others were at Millwall and Tilbury and, as in Part One, full details of each engine appear only under its original location and owner, with its subsequent movements listed in its personal history.

Having reached a peak in the 1950s, trade at the docks began to decline in the 1960s due to several factors, principally, the size of vessels and the move to containerisation. Closure of the docks began in 1968 at St Katharine's and the Surrey Commercial fell victim soon afterwards in 1970. With the downturn in cargo and increasing road haulage, the PLA closed its internal rail system on 1st May 1970. The India & Millwall Docks had succumbed to closure in 1980 and the Royal Docks ceased to operate just a year later, being host to ghostly laid up ships for a further two years.

1981 heralded the arrival of The London Docklands Development Corporation (LDDC) to oversee the regeneration of the area. While the India & Millwall became the capital's centre of finance, the Royal Docks underwent a metamorphosis as the London City Airport.

During the course of this book abbreviations are given for several locomotive manufacturers. Their full details are as follows:

AB Andrew Barclay Sons & Co Ltd, Caledonia Works, Kilmarnock, Ayrshire
AE Avonside Engine Co Ltd, Fishponds, Bristol
AP Aveling & Porter Ltd, Invicta Works, Rochester, Kent
BEV British Electric Vehicles Ltd, Southport
Bg E E Baguley Ltd, Burton on Trent, Staffordshire
BH Black, Hawthorn & Co Ltd, Gateshead
BLW Baldwin Locomotive Works, Philadelphia, USA
Bton London Brighton & South Coast Railway, Brighton Works, Sussex
Crewe London & North Western Railway, Crewe Works, Cheshire
D Dubs & Co Ltd, Polmadie Works, Glasgow
Dav Davenport Locomotive Works, Davenport, USA
Dec Societe Nouvelle des Establishments Decauville Aine, Petit Bourg, Corbeil, Essonne, France
EB E Borrows & Sons, St Helens, Lancashire
FE Falcon Engine Works, Loughborough, Leicestershire
FH F C Hibberd & Co Ltd, Park Royal, London
FW Fox Walker & Co Ltd, Atlas Engine Works, Bristol
GWR Great Western Railway, Swindon Works
H James & Fredk Howard Ltd, Britannia Ironworks, Bedford
HC Hudswell, Clarke & Co Ltd, Railway Foundry, Leeds
HE Hunslet Engine Co Ltd, Hunslet, Leeds
HH Henry Hughes & Company, Falcon Works, Loughborough
HL R & W Hawthorn, Leslie & Co Ltd, Forth Bank Works, Newcastle-upon-Tyne
Hor Lancashire & Yorkshire Railway, Horwich Works, Lancashire
JF John Fowler & Co (Leeds) Ltd, Hunslet, Leeds
KS Kerr, Stewart & Co Ltd, California Works, Stoke on Trent
LNWR London & North Western Railway, Crewe Works
Long R B Longridge & Co, Bedlington, Northumberland
MW Manning, Wardle & Co, Ltd, Boyne Engine Works, Leeds
MR Motor Rail Ltd, Simplex Works, Bedford
N Neilson & Co Ltd, Springburn Works, Glasgow
P Peckett & Sons Ltd, Atlas Locomotive Works, Bristol
RB Redpath Brown Ltd, Greenwich
RH Ruston & Hornsby Ltd, Lincoln
RP Ruston, Proctor & Co Ltd, Sheaf Iron Works, Lincoln
RR Rolls-Royce Ltd, Sentinel Works, Shrewsbury
RS Robert Stephenson & Co Ltd, Forth Street, Newcastle-upon-Tyne
RSH Robert Stephenson & Hawthorns Ltd, Newcastle-upon-Tyne
RSHN Robert Stephenson & Hawthorns Ltd, Forth Banks Works, Newcastle-upon-Tyne
S Sentinel (Shrewsbury) Ltd, Battlefield Works, Shrewsbury
Sdn Great Western Railway, Swindon Works
Shanks Alexander Shanks & Son Ltd, Dens Iron Works, Arbroath
SS Sharp Stewart & Co, Atlas Works, Manchester & Glasgow
TH Thomas Hill (Rotherham) Ltd, Vanguard Works, Kilnhurst, South Yorkshire
TG T Green & Son Ltd, Leeds
VF Vulcan Foundry Ltd, Newton le Willows, Lancashire
WB W G Bagnall Ltd, Castle Engine Works, Stafford.
WSO Wellman Smith Owen Engineering Corporation Ltd, Darlaston, Staffordshire
YE Yorkshire Engine Co Ltd, Meadow Hall Works, Sheffield

CHAPTER 1

The Victoria Docks

Following the huge successes of the East and West India Docks, the Victoria Dock Company was formed in 1850 and set about building its own docks on Plaistow Marshes to a design that would admit much larger vessels than its rivals. The Victoria Docks covered some 90 acres when the huge basin was opened by Prince Albert on 26th November 1855. It was London's first dock designed expressly for steamships and was equipped with the latest hydraulic machinery and cranes.

Primarily intended for the meat trade, the estate provided numerous cold stores to hold produce from South America. There were facilities for the transportation and storage of fruit, bananas and tobacco, and this was the first of the London docks to be planned with direct rail access from the main line to its quaysides.

The Eastern Counties and Thames Junction Railway to North Woolwich had opened on 14th June 1847 and paved the way for some urbanisation of the area but the entrance to the dock, near Bow Creek, was constructed along its route. During the early works a swing bridge was built to carry the line over the lock but it was soon realised this would present problems to both the railway and the shipping companies with constant delays to movements of both parties' traffic. This led to the line being rerouted along the north and east of the dock by the time of the dock's opening (see the chapter on the North Woolwich Railway).

The new line rejoined its former route at Silvertown and continued along to North Woolwich but the old section of the railway between Bugsby's Reach (the original swing bridge) and Silvertown was taken over by the dock company and retained to serve several factories along its course. This later became known as the Silvertown Tramway.

During its formative years the docks was served by locomotives from the Eastern Counties Railway (later part of the Great Eastern) and stations for dock workers were built at Custom House and Tidal Basin in 1855 and 1858 respectively. Sidings to the north quay connected to the main line at Tidal Basin while a branch to the south quay joined to the original line south of the Bow Creek swing bridge.

Up river, near the city, the St Katharine Dock and the London Dock companies had been casting envious glances at the new era dock enterprises. Their own cramped facilities were now inadequate for the modern ships, especially as sail had turned to steam and, having formed an amalgamation as the London & St Katharine Dock Company in 1864, they launched a successful bid to take over the Victoria Dock Company just two years later.

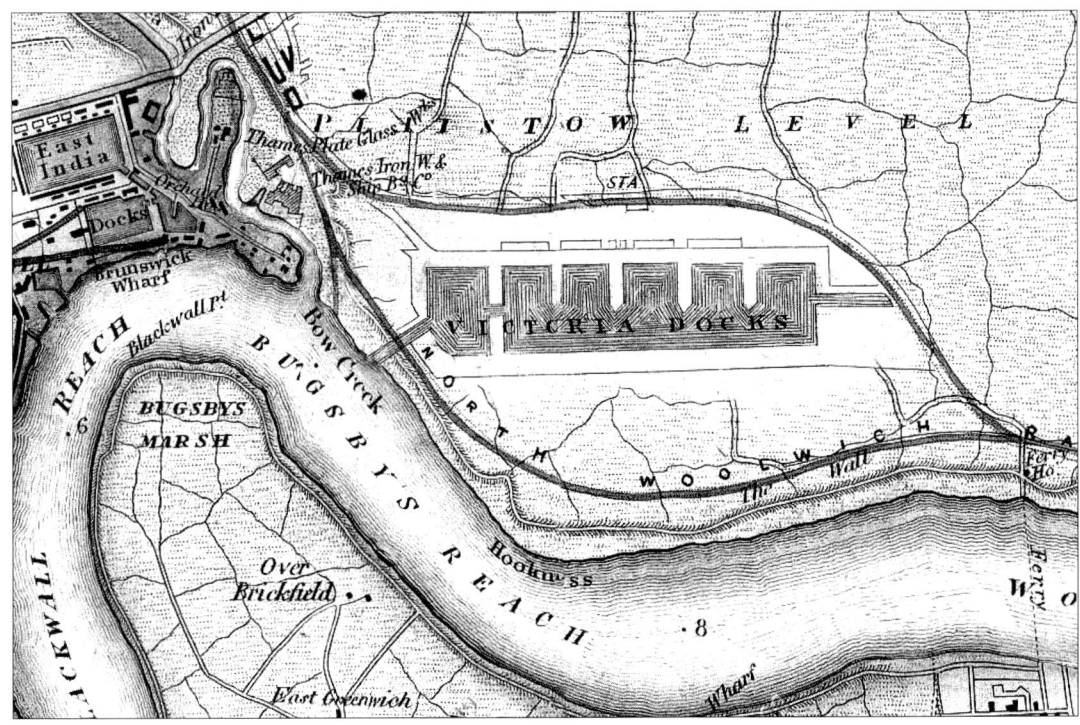

An early, though slightly inaccurate map of the Victoria Docks showing both the original and revised routes of the North Woolwich Railway. (Author's Collection)

London's Dock Railways: The Royal Docks, North Woolwich and Silvertown

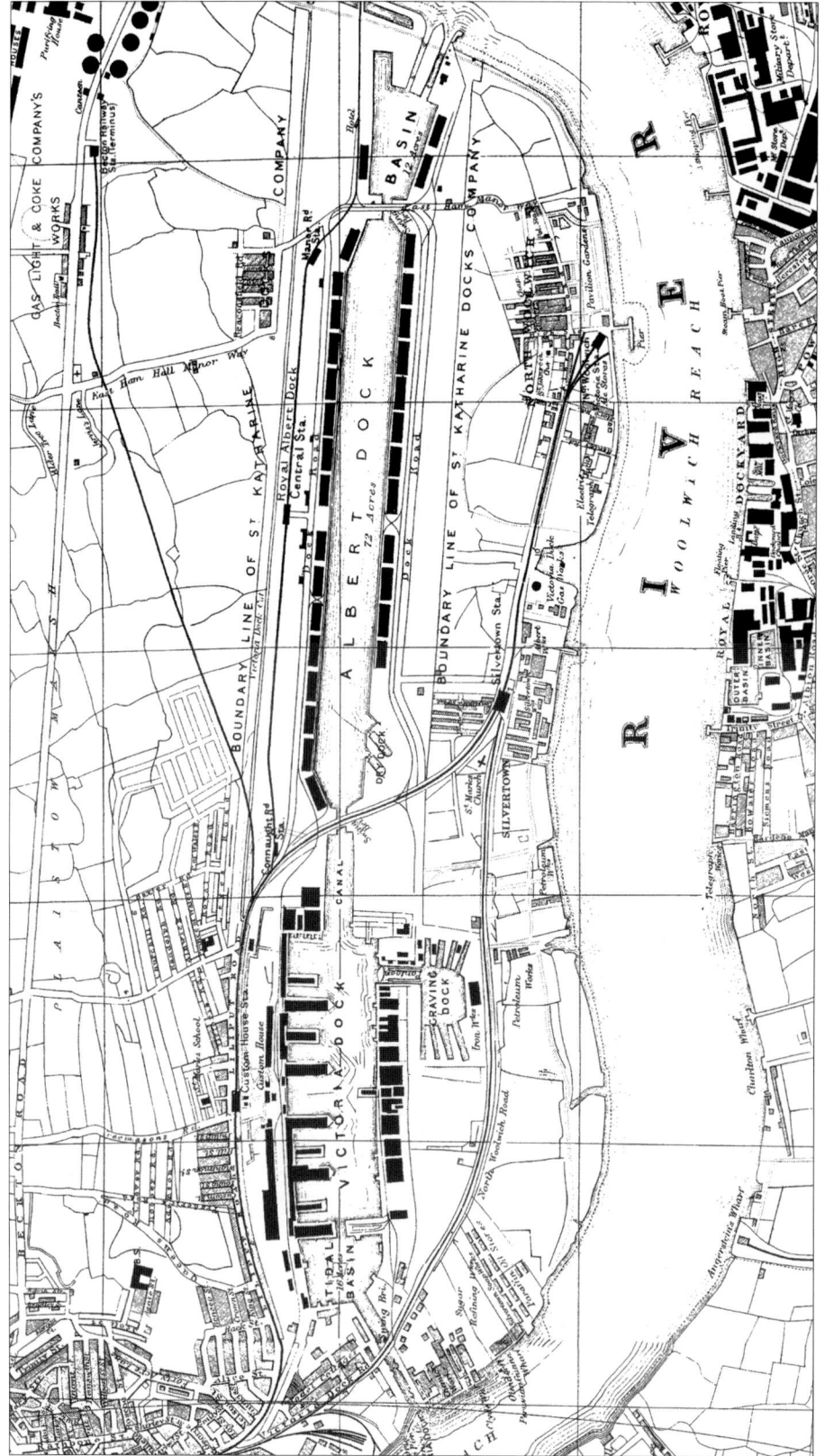

The Royal Docks in 1888 showing the original and revised route of the North Woolwich Railway to north and south of the Victoria Dock. (Author's Collection)

CHAPTER 2

The Victoria and Albert Docks

The two dock companies of St Katharine and London Docks had found themselves somewhat left behind in the wake of the new docks that had materialised down river where facilities could accommodate much bigger vessels at spacious quays with larger warehouses. By combining forces as the London & St Katharine Dock Company in 1864 they were able to purchase the relatively new Victoria Docks when that company encountered financial difficulties in 1866.

The new establishment enjoyed great prosperity before expanding the Victoria Dock eastwards with the construction of the Albert Dock that could accommodate vessels up to 12,000 tons, the two docks being connected by a short canal known as the Connaught Passage which, once again, crossed the path of the previously rerouted North Woolwich Railway. This threatened to pose the same dilemma as before with a clash of interests between ships and railway. The problem was alleviated by the construction of a tunnel under the cut, completed in 1878 ahead of the opening of the 72 acre Albert Dock. The ceremony was performed on the 24th June 1880 by the Duke and Duchess of Connaught when the title "Royal" was appended, after which the Victoria Dock was also afforded that distinction.

The L&StKD Co's first locos were two 0-4-0 saddle tanks purchased second hand in December 1878, arriving the following month. These were a pair from four Shanks-built locomotives that were auctioned on the quayside at Southampton Docks after returning from a harbour works contract at Cuxhaven in Germany. A third loco went to the Millwall Docks around the same time. The two Royal Docks locos ran in black livery and were given the appropriate names *Victoria* and *Albert* although they were commonly referred to as "*The Scotchmen*" by their crews.

The contract for the construction of the Albert Dock had been let to the firm of Lucas & Aird who used at least a dozen locos in the works while employing around 700 wagons for the removal of earth. Two of their engines were subsequently leased to the Dock Company, one named *Chelsea* and the other known as *Long Wind*. Both were 0-6-0 saddle tanks and were possibly used as the initial motive power on the Royal Albert Dock Passenger Railway in 1880 (see that chapter). *Long Wind* was described as "made up from odd parts of scrapped locos". Its firebox, sitting less than 3 inches above rail level, suggested the loco might have had larger driving wheels in a previous existence. On 8th February 1881 a huge fire broke out at No 5 shed in the Victoria Docks where buildings, cargoes, barges and railway trucks were destroyed. The heat was so intense it buckled railway tracks and both *Chelsea* and *Long Wind* were severely damaged as the wooden shed in which they were housed burned down. Following repairs, they were purchased by the L&StKD Co but, while *Long Wind* was retained, *Chelsea* had been disposed of in that year.

About that time, thought was given to increasing the locomotive stock. A three-road running shed capable of housing 16-18 locos was built at Custom House while maintenance workshops were erected nearby a little later. Four new locos, numbers 1438 –1441, from makers Dubs & Co, were purchased in 1881. These arrived in green livery and had been originally designed for a foreign customer in sunnier climes; their open cabs were totally unsuited to the rigours of the East London weather. Nevertheless they were very popular with overcoated crews. Their main dimensions were:

Cylinders: 15in x 20in
Driving Wheels: 3ft 6in
Boiler Pressure: 120psi
Wheelbase: 8ft 0in

They were all rebuilt in 1901 and given new boilers pressured at 130psi before being sent back to work in black livery and giving many more useful years of service.

Also in 1881, three former London & North Western Railway 2-4-0 tank engines arrived to work the Royal Albert Dock Passenger Railway as replacements for *Long Wind* and *Chelsea*. These were purchased second hand from the railway company and had originally been tender engines running in the northern division of the L&NWR. They became L&StKD Co numbers 5 –7 and operated the line to Gallions. The next arrivals were three Fox Walker engines, numbers 149, 288 and 263, second hand from contractor John Dickson Jnr of Liverpool between 1882 and 1883, along with a Yorkshire Engine Co 0-4-0ST No 284, also in 1883.

The loco stock running number series at Custom House was then numbers 1– 4 the Dubs engines, numbers 5– 7 the ex-LNWR locos on the Royal Albert

3

Dock Passenger Service, number 8 *Long Wind* the Longridge engine, numbers 9 and 10 the two Shanks *Victoria* and *Albert*, numbers 11−13 the three Fox Walkers and number 14 the Yorkshire Engine Co loco.

In 1884 the L&StKD Co began extending the Royal Albert Dock, making it some one and a quarter miles long. The project commenced in May and included the construction of a new entrance lock and enlargement of the Gallions Basin. In doing so, the company purchased six locos which it employed in the works. These were an odd assortment of engines from a variety of makers. Firstly, there were new arrivals from Manning Wardle (numbers 893 and 905), along with Hunslet number 343, and a neat little engine from the Falcon Engineering Co (works number unknown). Also unnumbered was a second-hand Ruston Proctor engine and, finally, a converted former tram engine from Falcon. One of the dock company's existing Shanks locos, *Albert*, was also employed in the scheme. The Ruston Proctor engine was painted in red livery and thought also to have originally also been a tram engine. It had a left-handed regulator which almost caused an accident shortly after its arrival.

The principal works were completed by May 1886 and the company scheduled an auction on 12th October 1887 for the disposal of machinery, including six 0-4-0 saddle tanks, but it would appear that all were subsequently retained and absorbed into the Royal Docks locomotive stock. The running order then became 1−8 and 11−14 as before, with the two Shanks locos renumbered to 16 and 17. MW 905 was now number 9 the Hunslet was given number 10, the Falcon became number 15, the Ruston Proctor was then number 18 and the tram engine number 20; but what of number 19? Logic suggests this would have been MW number 893, which ran as number 16 after *Victoria* was sold in 1896.

The compliment at Custom House remained thus until darker days saw the majority of the docks undertakings fall under the administration umbrella of the London & India Docks Joint Committee on 1st January 1889.

London & St Katherine Dock Company 0-4-0ST Shanks Number not known

Name:	*Victoria, (James Godwin)*
Manufacturer:	Alexander Shanks & Son Ltd
Built:	1870
Running number:	No 9 (L&StKD Co), No 16 (both L&StKD Co and L&IDJC)
Cylinders:	10in x 20in
Driving Wheels:	3ft 1in
Wheelbase:	5ft 6in
Weight:	18ton 7.5 cwt
At the Docks:	1879 − 1896

One of two locomotives purchased by the London & St Katharine Dock Company from Southampton Docks Engineer Alfred Giles, being one of four that had worked for him at Cuxhaven Harbour and were afterwards sold by auction at Southampton. With sister engine *Albert* it had arrived in 1879 and carried the number 9 until renumbered as 16 in 1884. *Victoria's* stay was shorter than that of *Albert*, having been sold in 1896 to the Stonecourt Chalk, Lime & Pier Company Ltd at Dartford in Kent where it was reportedly renamed *James Godwin* and afterwards sold to a firm in Portland.

The Victoria and Albert Docks

London & St Katharine Dock Company 0-4-0ST Shanks Number not known

Name:	*Albert*
Manufacturer:	Alexander Shanks & Son Ltd
Built:	1872
Running number:	No 10 (L&StKD Co), No 17 (L&StKD Co L&IDJC and L&ID Co)
Cylinders:	10in x 20in
Driving Wheels:	3ft 1in
Wheelbase:	5ft 6in
Weight:	18ton 7.5 cwt
At the Docks:	1879 – 1902

The second of two Shanks locomotives purchased second hand from Southampton Docks Engineer Alfred Giles, also being one of a quartet that previously had worked for him on the construction of Cuxhaven Harbour (a third Shanks loco went to Millwall Docks). With sister engine *Victoria* it arrived in 1879 and they became the first two locomotives acquired by the London & St Katharine Dock Company. *Albert* worked on the Royal Albert Dock extension works and carried the number 10 until 1884 when it was renumbered 17. Not much is recorded of either locos' time in the docks except that *Albert* had been transferred to the West India Docks around 1889 but by 1891 was laid up outside the South Dock shed and partly dismantled, remaining in this state until sold for scrap in 1902. Reportedly, *Albert* was removed on a GCR horse drawn wagon to Marylebone station and bound for a firm in the north.

Shanks loco "Albert", pictured outside the South Dock shed, West India Docks in 1901, prior to its disposal. (Frank Jones Collection/Industrial Locomotive Society)

London & St Katharine Dock Company 0-6-0ST Longridge

Name:	*(Long Wind)*
Manufacturer:	R B Longridge & Co
Built:	1847 (Rebuilt LBSCR 1860 and 1865)
Running number:	75, 104 (both LB&SCR), 8 (both L&StKD Co and L&IDJC)
Cylinders:	16in x 24in
Driving Wheels:	4ft 8in
Boiler Pressure:	120psi
Wheelbase:	14ft 0in
At the Docks:	1880 – 1898

Built by R B Longridge as a tender engine in October 1847, this loco was one of eight such designs supplied to the LB&SCR for goods traffic. The engine was rebuilt in 1860 and again in 1865 when converted to a saddle tank at Brighton Works. Its service with the railway company ended in September 1870 when it was sold to contractor George Wythes who employed it on his construction works for Millwall Docks. Further use came when sent to other harbour works at Sharpness in the Bristol Channel in January 1871 where that contract ran until 1873, after which it was purchased by fellow contractors John Aird who were then building the railway extension to Portsmouth Harbour. While there it was repaired by the LB&SCR in 1875 and resumed work at Portsmouth until 1876 when Aird brought the loco back to London during the construction of the Royal Albert Docks. According to *The Locomotive* magazine edition of January 1902 it had worked alongside another ancient loco named *Chelsea* and, at the end of the contract, both locos were loaned to the L&StKD Co in 1880 for use on the Royal Albert Dock Passenger Railway. They were housed in a wooden shed which burnt down in 1881 causing considerable damage to both. However, the Dock Company repaired both engines but the new partnership was short lived as *Chelsea* was soon disposed of. The old Longridge loco, often referred to by its nickname of *Long Wind*, was purchased outright by the docks in 1881 and ran as their No 8 but reportedly suffered damage when derailed after running down an incline near Custom House. It was then sold to a firm in the north of England and, having been despatched to the L&NWR goods yard in Carlisle in 1898, it was scrapped in 1901.

An enlightening photo of the L&StKD Co No 8 shows this powerful engine's features. (Author's Collection)

The Victoria and Albert Docks

London & St Katharine Dock Company 0-6-0ST LB&SCR

Name:	*Chelsea*
Manufacturer:	London Brighton & South Coast Railway
Built:	1865
Cylinders:	16in x 24in
Driving Wheels:	4ft 8in
Boiler Pressure:	120psi
Wheelbase:	14ft 0in
At the Docks:	1880 – 1881

Not a great deal is known about this loco, which arrived during the construction of the Albert Docks under the ownership of contractors Lucas & Aird. It is thought to have been previously engaged in works at Portsmouth, possibly alongside the Longridge engine known as *Long Wind*, and perhaps arrived in London at the same time in 1876. Both engines were loaned to the Dock Company in 1880 for use on the Royal Albert Dock Passenger Railway and, having suffered considerable damage by fire in 1881, the locos were repaired by the L&StKD Co. Whereas *Long Wind* was purchased by them, *Chelsea* was scrapped after a short time.

There was also an alternative story suggesting that *Chelsea* may have been Manning Wardle No 608 built in 1876 which, according to one unsubstantiated report, was purchased by the L&StKD Co in 1881. This 0-6-0ST had 12in x 17in inside cylinders and at one time belonged to Lucas & Aird but it was not listed as being at the Albert Dock contract and was later recorded as working on the Manchester Sheffield and Lincolnshire Railway in 1884.

London & St Katharine Dock Company 0-6-0ST Dubs No 1438

Manufacturer:	Dubs & Co Ltd
Built:	1881
Works number:	1438
Running number:	No 1 (L&StKD Co, L&IDJC, L&ID Co and PLA)
At the Docks:	1881 – 1917

New to the Royal Docks in 1881, this loco was rebuilt in 1901 and served all its time there, becoming part of the PLA fleet in 1909 and eventually being laid aside as a source of spares in 1917, the remains being disposed of by 1920.

One of the four Dubs locos was shown at Custom House shed in The Locomotive Magazine published in December 1901. Although poor quality, the photograph does illustrate the pleasing lines of these engines. (Author's Collection)

London's Dock Railways: The Royal Docks, North Woolwich and Silvertown

London & St Katharine Dock Company 0-6-0ST Dubs No 1439

Manufacturer:	Dubs & Co Ltd
Built:	1881
Works number:	1439
Running number:	No 2 (L&StKD Co, L&IDJC, L&ID Co and PLA)
At the Docks:	1881−1920

Second of the quartet supplied new from Dubs & Co arriving at the Royal Docks in 1881. Having been rebuilt in 1901 it survived into PLA ownership in 1909 and was transferred to the West India Docks during World War One. Upon return it lasted until sold in 1920.

London & St Katharine Dock Company 0-6-0ST Dubs No 1440

Manufacturer:	Dubs & Co Ltd
Built:	1881
Works number:	1440
Running number:	No 3 (L&StKD Co, L&IDJC, L&ID Co and PLA)
At the Docks:	1881 − 1917

This was the third of four locos supplied new to the Royal Docks in 1881. Like the others, it was rebuilt in 1901 and survived into the PLA era in 1909. Along with sister No 1438 it was laid aside for spares in 1917 with the remains sold for scrap in 1920.

The elegant features of Dubs No 1439 are evident in this photo of the locomotive as London & St Katharine Dock Company No 2. The somewhat flimsy cab offered little protection against the elements. (Frank Jones Collection/ Industrial Locomotive Society)

The Victoria and Albert Docks

London & St Katharine Dock Company 0-6-0ST Dubs No 1441

Manufacturer:	Dubs & Co Ltd
Built:	1881
Works number:	1441
Running number:	No 4 (L&StKD Co, L&IDJC, L&ID Co and PLA)
At the Docks:	1881 – 1920

The last of four locos from Dubs & Co supplied new to the Royal Docks in 1881. As with the other three it was rebuilt in 1901 and worked into the PLA takeover before being sold, with No 1439 in 1920.

London & St Katharine Dock Company 0-6-0ST Fox Walker No 149

Name:	*(Halifax)*
Manufacturer:	Fox Walker & Co Ltd
Built:	1872
Works number:	149
Running number:	No 11 (L&StKD Co and L&IDJC), No 11A (L&ID Co and PLA)
Cylinders:	13in x 20in
Driving Wheels:	3ft 6in
Boiler Pressure:	120psi
Wheelbase:	9ft 9in
At the Docks:	1882 – 1913

This engine was originally supplied new in 1872 to a Halifax contractor, T J Waller, and was appropriately named *Halifax*. Waller used the loco in his works on the Halifax & Overden Junction Railway and later during the construction of the Chatburn to Hellifield line for the Lancashire and Yorkshire Railway. The loco then found its way to another contractor by the name of John Dickson Jnr, at his Alexandra Dock contract in Liverpool around 1874 after which it was sold to the London & St Katharine Dock Company at the Royal Docks in June 1882. Under the subsequent ownership of the London & India Docks Company, the loco was rebuilt in 1901 and then transferred to the East & West India Docks on loan from 3rd October that year until returning in October 1903. In 1902 it had been renumbered 11A due to duplication. After becoming part of the PLA stock in 1909 it was reportedly the victim of a boiler explosion in 1912 and afterwards sold for scrap to dealers George Cohen Sons & Co around 1913.

London & St Katharine Dock Company 0-6-0ST Fox Walker No 288

Manufacturer:	Fox Walker & Co Ltd
Built:	30th November 1875
Works number:	288
Running number:	No 12 (L&StKD Co and L&IDJC), 12A (L&ID Co and PLA)
Cylinders:	13in x 20in
Driving Wheels:	3ft 6in
Wheelbase:	9ft 9in
Boiler Pressure:	120psi
At the Docks:	1883 – 1913

FW 288 was new to C Tottenham at their Alexandra Docks contract in Liverpool and, along with sister No 263, moved to fellow contractor John Dickson Jnr, also of Liverpool, in 1882 and the pair were purchased second hand by the London & St Katharine Dock Co in October 1883 for use in the Royal Docks. Running as No 12 it was transferred to the East & West India Docks in 1901, where, because of duplication, it was renumbered to 12A by the London & India Dock Company. While at the West India Docks it was noted on the Millwall Extension Railway on the 30th March 1903 before returning to the Royal Docks later that year. Having survived into PLA days it was transferred back to the West India Docks in 1911, working there until withdrawn in 1912, after which it remained idle at the South Dock shed along with *Bee* (HE No 235) and *Swift* (JF No 3807) until all three were sold for scrap to dealer George Cohen Sons & Co in the following year.

Fox Walker engine No 288 pictured as London and India Docks Joint Committee No 12. (Frank Jones Collection/ Industrial Locomotive Society)

The Victoria and Albert Docks

London & St Katharine Dock Company 0-6-0ST Fox Walker No 263

Manufacturer:	Fox Walker & Co Ltd
Built:	1875
Works number:	263
Running number:	No 13 (L&StKD Co, L&IDJC, L&ID Co and PLA)
Cylinders:	13in x 20in
Driving Wheels:	3ft 6in
Wheelbase:	9ft 9in
Boiler Pressure:	120psi
At the Docks:	1883 – 1917

Having been dispatched new from the makers to the firm of C Tottenham of Liverpool in 1875 this loco had found its way to neighbouring contractor John Dickson Jnr in 1882 and was later sold to the London & St Katharine Docks Company, along with FW No 288, in October 1883. Unlike its two sisters (numbers 149 and 288), it was not transferred to the India Docks but remained at the Royal Docks where it was kept as a spare engine for the Royal Albert Dock Passenger Railway, and eventually worked on into PLA days until sold for scrap to George Cohen Sons & Co in 1917.

A smart Fox Walker No 263 poses as London & India Joint Committee No 13. (Frank Jones Collection / Industrial Locomotive Society)

London & St Katharine Dock Company 0-4-0ST Yorkshire No 284

Name:	*(Rutland)*
Manufacturer:	Yorkshire Engine Co Ltd
Built:	1876
Works number:	284
Running number:	14 (L&StKD Co, L&IDJC, L&ID Co and PLA)
Cylinders:	12in x 20in
Driving Wheels:	3ft 3in
Wheelbase:	5ft 9in
Boiler Pressure:	120psi
Water capacity	420galls
Coal capacity:	12cwt
Weight:	21ton 0cwt
At the Docks:	1883 – 1917

A loco with solid cast iron wheels which was new to contractors Benton & Woodiwiss in 1876. Naming it *Rutland* they employed it on their contract for the Great Northern Railway's Marefield Junction to Leicester line before selling it to the London & St Katherine Dock Co around 1883. One source suggests it possibly spent some time at the West India Docks. After surviving into PLA days in 1909 it worked on until sold in 1917.

The driver of YE No 284 looked a little apprehensive when photographed aboard L&IDJC's No 14 at Custom House. (John Alsop Collection)

The Victoria and Albert Docks

London & St Katharine Dock Company 0-4-0ST Falcon Number not known

Manufacturer:	Falcon Engine & Car Works Ltd
Built:	1884
Running number:	No 15 (L&StKD Co, L&IDJC, L&ID Co and PLA)
Cylinders:	9in x 15in
Driving Wheels:	2ft 6in
Boiler Pressure:	120psi
At the Docks:	1884 – 1914

One of six locomotives that began life on the London & St Katharine Dock Company's works for the extension of the Royal Albert Dock where this Falcon engine was supplied new in 1884. After the project ended in October 1887 it became part of the Royal Albert Docks fleet, carrying the number 15 into the administration days of the Joint Committee and also the PLA era before being sold in 1914.

The driver of this petite Falcon Engineering loco, L&IDJC No 15, looks a little less anxious than when pictured aboard YE No 284 at Custom House (see opposite). (John Alsop Collection)

London & St Katharine Dock Company 0-4-0ST Manning Wardle No 893

Name:	*(Minnie)*
Manufacturer:	Manning, Wardle & Co Ltd
Built:	2nd December 1884
Works number:	893
Running number:	?No 19 and 16 (both L&StKD Co and L&IDJC)
Cylinders:	8in x 14in
Driving Wheels:	2ft 8in
Wheelbase:	4ft 6in
Boiler Pressure:	140psi
Tank capacity	200galls
Weight:	9ton 12cwt
At the Docks:	1884 – 1900

New from the makers, this was the L&StKD Co's first Manning Wardle engine, being one of a pair (the other was No 905) purchased for the dock company's works when extending the Royal Albert Docks from 1884 until the project was completed in October 1887. At that time its principal function was to haul a saloon showing VIPs around the works and, when those were completed, the saloon became a time office at Custom House. The loco was afterwards taken into the company fleet, possibly running as No 19, then becoming No 16 when that number became available after the Shanks engine *Victoria* was sold in 1896. Its time at Custom House lasted only until 1900 when sold to the firm of MacKay & Davies at Gloucester where it carried the name *Minnie* until meeting its end at an unknown date.

London & St Katharine Dock Company 0-4-0ST Manning Wardle No 905

Manufacturer:	Manning, Wardle & Co Ltd
Built:	27th August 1884
Works number:	905
Running number:	No 9 (L&StKD Co), No 16 (L&IDJC, L&ID Co, and PLA)
Cylinders:	12in x 18in
Driving Wheels:	3ft 0in
Wheelbase:	5ft 4in
Boiler Pressure:	120psi
Tank capacity	450galls
Weight:	19ton 17cwt
At the Docks:	1884 – 1920

Manning Wardle No 905 was supplied new to the London & St Katharine Dock Company where it was engaged in the company's works for the extension of the Royal Albert Docks. At the end of the contract in October 1887 it became absorbed into the company fleet at Custom House and later it worked under the London & India Docks Joint Committee from 1889, running as No 9 until renumbered to 16 after 1900 (in place of the departed MW No 893) when taken over by the London & India Docks Company. After further service with the PLA from 1909 it was eventually sold, possibly to the War Department, in 1920.

The Victoria and Albert Docks

London & St Katharine Dock Company 0-4-0ST Ruston Proctor Number not known

Manufacturer:	Ruston, Proctor & Co Ltd
Built:	1870
Running number:	No 18 (L&StKD Co, L&IDJC, L&ID Co and PLA)
Cylinders:	9in x 16in
Driving Wheels:	2ft 9in
Wheelbase:	5ft 6in
Boiler Pressure:	120psi
Weight:	16ton 11cwt
At the Docks:	1884 – 1912

This was a strange looking engine obtained second hand from an unknown source when purchased for work on the L&StKD Co's extension works to the Royal Albert Dock in 1884. As with the others involved, it was taken into the dock company fleet after the project finished in October 1887, surviving through to the receivership of the London & India Docks Joint Committee and then entering the PLA era in 1909. After that it was little used and for some while languished in the shed with a holed firebox in 1911 before being sold for scrap in 1912.

The odd-looking Ruston Proctor loco as L&IDJC No 18 pictured at the Royal Docks Custom House shed. (Jim Peden Collection/Industrial Railway Society)

Manning Wardle No 905 pictured at Custom House in its days as No 16 for the L&IDJC. (Author's Collection)

15

London & St Katharine Dock Company 0-4-0ST Hunslet No 343

Manufacturer:	Hunslet Engine Co Ltd
Built:	12th September 1884
Works number:	343
Running number:	No 10 (L&StKD Co and L&IDJC), No 19 (L&ID Co and PLA)
Cylinders:	13in x 18in
Driving Wheels:	3ft 1in
Wheelbase:	5ft 6in
Boiler Pressure:	120psi
At the Docks:	1884 – 1910

Delivered new to the London & St Katharine Dock Company for their Royal Albert Dock extension contract, Hunslet No 343 was retained for dock working after the works were completed in October 1887. Initially numbered 10, it was changed to 19 in 1901 when absorbed into the London & India Docks Company fleet. Having just made it into the PLA era it was in poor condition and scrapped in 1910.

Above: Hunslet No 343 poses in its London & India Docks Joint Committee livery. (Author's Collection)

Opposite page: This photograph shows a Hughes Locomotive and Tramway engine which was built around 1877 and illustrates the type of vehicle that may have been in use at the Albert Dock works. (Author's Collection)

The Victoria and Albert Docks

London & St Katharine Dock Company 0-4-0 Tram Falcon/Hughes Number not known

Name:	(Ajax)
Manufacturer:	Falcon Engine & Car Works Ltd
Built:	?1883
Running number:	No 20 (L&StKD Co and L&IDJC)
Cylinders:	7in x 12in
Driving Wheels:	2ft 6in
Wheelbase:	4ft 6in
At the Docks:	1884 – 1900

This tram engine was acquired by the dock company during extension works at the Royal Albert Dock which began in 1884 and were completed in 1887. Afterwards it appears to have been absorbed into the dock company fleet along with other locos from those works in October that year. Although recorded as built by Falcon, it may well have been a product of the Henry Hughes Tramway Engine Works which were taken over by Falcon in 1882. Falcon then sold off the remaining Hughes stock, possibly with new works plates under their own name. Such low powered engines were designed for slow speeds and equipped with condensing apparatus for operation on public roads. The fact this engine is recorded as a "converted" tram loco suggests it might have been stripped back to its basics for use in menial tasks around the construction site, such as towing a VIP inspection saloon. It was disposed of in 1900 to the firm of Clark & Standfield, who had engineering works at Grays in Essex, where it was possibly named *Ajax* and last recorded there in July of that year.

Locomotives purchased by the London & St Katharine Dock Company

Maker	Works No	Name	Type	Running No	Date Arrived	PLA Number	Date Departed	Notes	
D	1438		0-6-0ST	1	1881	1	1917		Scrapped for spares
D	1439		0-6-0ST	2	1881	2	1920		Sold
D	1440		0-6-0ST	3	1881	3	1917		Scrapped for spares
D	1441		0-6-0ST	4	1881	4	1920		Sold
Crewe	?		2-4-0T	5	1881	-	1896	RADPR	Sold for Scrap
Crewe	?		2-4-0T	6	1881	-	1896	RADPR	Sold for Scrap
Crewe	?		2-4-0T	7	1881	-	1896	RADPR	Sold for Scrap
Longridge	?	*Long Wind*	0-6-0ST	8	1880	-	1898		Sold
MW	905		0-4-0ST	9	1884	16	1920		Sold
HE	343		0-4-0ST	10	1884	19	1910		Scrapped
FW	149		0-6-0ST	11	1882	11A	1913		Sold for Scrap
FW	288		0-6-0ST	12	1883	12A	1913		Sold for Scrap
FW	263		0-6-0ST	13	1883	13	1917		Sold for Scrap
YE	284		0-4-0ST	14	1883	14	1917		Sold
FE	?		0-4-0ST	15	1884	15	1914		Sold
Shanks	?	*Victoria*	0-4-0ST	9/16	1879	-	1896		Sold
Shanks	?	*Albert*	0-4-0ST	10/17	1879	-	1902		Scrapped
RP	?		0-4-0ST	18	1884	18	1912		Sold for scrap
MW	893		0-4-0ST	?19/16	1883	-	1900		Sold
FE	?		0-4-0tram	20	1884	-	1900	Tram	Sold
Bton	?	*Chelsea*	0-6-0ST	-	1880	-	1881		Scrapped

RAPDR: Royal Albert Dock Passenger Railway

The London and India Docks Joint Committee had overseen the affairs of the East & West India Dock Company, along with those of the London & St Katharine Dock Company from 1st January 1889. The latter had sought to amalgamate with the Indias but that liaison was delayed until 1898 while, in the meantime, the two concerns continued to operate separately under the umbrella of the Joint Committee

One of the Committee's first acts was to review the wages of all railway staff at the Royal, Tilbury, and India Docks, bringing them into parity and setting new rates of pay from 2nd January 1890. This was for a six day week with overtime at the same rates and all were provided with uniforms which, in the case of shunters, consisted of cloth cap and jacket, with cord vest and trousers.

- Goods Foreman received 30 shillings a week during their first year of service, rising to 32 shillings and sixpence in the second year, and to 35 shillings after three years.
- Head Shunters were paid 28/- 29/- and 30/- respectively
- Shunters 25/- 26/- and 27/-
- Head Porters on passenger lines 24/- 25/- and 26/-
- Signalmen and Bridgemen 23/- 24/- and 25/-
- Gatemen 22/- 23/- and 24/-

At the start of the Joint Committee administration the full allocation at the Royal Docks was:

No 1 Dubs No 1438
No 2 Dubs No 1439
No 3 Dubs No 1440
No 4 Dubs No 1441
No 5 LNWR No 1819
No 6 LNWR No 1927
No 7 LNWR No 1911
No 8 Long No 104
No 9 MW No 905
No 10 HE No 343
No 11 FW No 149
No 12 FW No 288
No 13 FW No 263
No 14 YE No 284
No 15 FE
No 16 Shanks *Victoria*
No 17 Shanks *Albert*

The Victoria and Albert Docks

No 18 RP
No 19 MW 893
No 20 FE Tram

Under the administration years of the Joint Committee, several changes in loco stock at the Royal Docks came about in 1896. The three engines on the Royal Albert Dock Passenger Railway were now well past their best after having existed for half a century. A decision was made to hand over the motive power of the line to the GER and the ex-LNWR engines were withdrawn and relegated to a few menial shunting duties before being sold for scrap to George Cohen Sons & Co at nearby Canning Town. The Shanks loco *Victoria* was also sold in that year, while 1898 saw the departure of the Longridge engine *Long Wind* after it had sustained damage in a derailment. Manning Wardle No 893, which had seen only a comparatively short time at Custom House was sold off in 1900, a year which also saw the departure of the Falcon tram engine.

Correspondingly, 1896 saw the appearance of larger and more powerful engines at Custom House with Robert Stephenson numbers 2844 and 2845 being the first of five new 0-6-0 saddle tanks, the first pair were purchased at a cost of £1245 each, with the other trio, numbers 2981–3, arriving by 1900, costing £1735 apiece. The first four were given the running numbers 5–8 in place of the departed engines, while the last one carried No 9 after MW No 905 was renumbered to 16 in 1900. The new engines must have been impressive as three more (numbers 3070, 3050 and 3094) were ordered by the succeeding London & India Docks Company which took over in 1901. The main dimensions of these were:

Cylinders:	16in x 20in
Driving Wheels:	3ft 6in
Boiler Pressure:	120psi
Water capacity:	800galls
Wheelbase:	8ft 0in
Weight:	34ton 10cwt

Stephenson No 2844 as PLA No 5 pictured at the Royal Victoria Docks in the 1930s. (Frank Jones Collection/ Industrial Locomotive Society)

London & India Docks Joint Committee Royal Docks 0-6-0ST Stephenson No 2844

Manufacturer: Robert Stephenson & Co Ltd
Built: 2nd October 1896
Works number: 2844
Running number: No 5 (L&IDJC, L&ID Co and PLA)
At the Docks: 1896–1937

The first of five new locos from this maker ordered by the London & India Docks Joint Committee between 1896 and 1900 (a further three followed in 1901–2 for the London & India Docks Co). No 2844 was dispatched to the Royal Docks on 2nd October 1896 and, like all its sisters, survived well into the PLA era. It was rebuilt in 1915 and worked on until 1929 when it was transferred to the East India Docks on 30th April that year by traversing the LNER tracks across Bow Creek. After returning to Custom House it was mostly idle until sold to dealers George Cohen Sons & Co at Canning Town on 29th July 1937 for £150. Cohens removed the loco on 8th October that year and they, in turn, sold it to the Lanarkshire Steel Company Ltd at Motherwell after which it went to nearby Colvilles Ltd at their Dalzell Works. A final move to Colvilles Clyde Ironworks at Glasgow came about before being scrapped in 1951. (See previous page for an illustration of this locomotive.)

London & India Docks Joint Committee Royal Docks 0-6-0ST Stephenson No 2845

Manufacturer: Robert Stephenson & Co Ltd
Built: 6th October 1896
Works number: 2845
Running number: No 6 (L&IDJC, L&ID Co and PLA)
At the Docks: 1896–1926

The second Stephenson loco to arrive in 1896 was also new from the makers. As with all its sisters it survived well into the PLA years, having been rebuilt by the docks based firm of Harland & Wolff in 1915. But by 1920 it was past its best and had been relegated to light duties. Having been withdrawn in 1925, it was then laid up at Custom House for a while before being broken up there in 1926.

London & India Docks Joint Committee Royal Docks 0-6-0ST Stephenson No 2981

Manufacturer: Robert Stephenson & Co Ltd
Built: 23rd May 1900
Works number: 2981
Running number: No 7 (L&IDJC, L&ID Co and PLA)
At the Docks: 1900–1929

The third of five Stephenson locomotives supplied new to the L&IDJC for work in the Royal Docks, the others being numbers 2844, 2845, 2982 and 2983, all in red livery and having copper topped chimneys. This loco was rebuilt in 1917 and gave several more years of service before its advancing years saw it used sparingly until it was noted out of use on 15th May 1929. Having been sold for scrap in August that year it was cut up in 1930.

The Victoria and Albert Docks

Stephenson No 2845 appeared to be well weathered when this photo was taken at the Custom House maintenance works. (Frank Jones Collection/Industrial Locomotive Society)

A very poor but rare photo of RS No 2981 as PLA No 7 at the Royal Docks. (Frank Jones Collection/Industrial Locomotive Society)

London & India Docks Joint Committee Royal Docks 0-6-0ST Stephenson No 2982

Name: *Agenor*

Manufacturer: Robert Stephenson & Co Ltd

Built: 28th May 1900

Works number: 2982

Running number: No 8 (L&IDJC and L&ID Co), 20 (PLA)

At the Docks: 1900–1934

The fourth of a batch of the five new locos supplied by this maker, having been purchased by the L&IDJC for employment at the Royal Docks and numbered 8. It was renumbered 20 and then transferred to Tilbury Docks in 1912 where it carried the name *Agenor*. At Tilbury it was rebuilt in 1924 and ran there until 1934 when sold to dealers Thomas W Ward Ltd. However, it remained idle there for sometime as Ward's sought to sell it on. After being viewed by two perspective buyers it disappeared soon after 15th January that year to Ward's premises at Columbia Wharf, Grays, where it was presumably broken up.

London & India Docks Joint Committee Royal Docks 0-6-0ST Stephenson No 2983

Manufacturer: Robert Stephenson & Co Ltd

Built: 31st May 1900

Works number: 2983

Running number: No 9 (L&IDJC, L&ID Co and PLA)

At the Docks: 1900–1926

The last of the five new Stephenson locos purchased by the L&IDJC for the Royal Docks. It underwent a rebuild by Harland & Wolff in 1915, working on until put up for sale in 1925. Unfortunately, no buyer was found and it was sold for scrap in November 1926

Stephenson No 2983 as a not so immaculate PLA No 9 at the Custom House maintenance works. (Frank Jones Collection/Industrial Locomotive Society)

The Victoria and Albert Docks

Stephenson No 2982 as L&IDJC No 8 at Custom House. (John Alsop Collection)

Locomotives purchased by the London & India Docks Joint Committee at Royal Docks

Maker	Works No	Name	Type	Running No	Date Arrived	PLA Number	Date Departed	Notes
RS	2844		0-6-0ST	5	1896	5	1937	Sold
RS	2845		0-6-0ST	6	1896	6	1926	Scrapped
RS	2981		0-6-0ST	7	1900	7	1929	Sold for scrap
RS	2982	*Agenor*	0-6-0ST	8	1900	8	1934	Sold
RS	2983		0-6-0ST	9	1900	9	1926	Sold for scrap

The London & India Docks Company had taken the majority of London's docks out of administration from under the Joint Committee from 1st January 1901. As owner of the India, Royal and Tilbury Docks it sought to address the ageing locomotive fleet with the introduction of new stock. The previous administration had already begun this process in its final years with five new 0-6-0ST engines from makers Robert Stephenson. The L&ID Co continued the sequence with three more of the same type with numbers 3050 and 3070 appearing in 1901 and No 3094 arriving in 1902. The Royal Docks fleet under the L&ID Co was made up as follows:

- The four Dubs locos numbers 1438–1441 (Running numbers 1–4)
- Stephensons 2844, 2845, 2981, 2982, 2983, 3050, 3070 and 3094 (5–12)
- Fox Walker numbers 149 (11A), 263 (12A) and 288 (13)
- Yorkshire Engine Co No 284 (14)
- The unnumbered Falcon (15)
- Manning Wardle No 905 (16)
- Ruston Proctor (18)
- Hunslet No 343 (19)

With the Stephenson locos well established, the Shanks loco *Albert* (No 17) had been sent to the West India Docks in 1889, and was followed there by Fox Walkers 288 and 149 in 1901, both FW locos returning in 1903. The Royal's railways had seen many changes over the past two decades but much more was to come as the new century unfolded and the docks entered its finest era with the formation of the Port of London Authority in 1909.

London & India Docks Company Royal Docks 0-6-0ST Stephenson No 3070

Manufacturer: Robert Stephenson & Co Ltd
Built: 25th February 1901
Works number: 3070
Running number: No 10 (L&ID Co and PLA)
At the Docks: 1901–1951

Sent new from the makers in 1901, No 3070 spent its formative years at the Royal Docks, being rebuilt there by the PLA in 1914 and again in 1921. From about 1930 it was periodically loaned to the West India Docks and on odd occasions worked the banana traffic at the East India Docks. During the Second World War it was again at the West India Docks from 12th August 1944, ending its days there when withdrawn in 1949 and sent for scrap to George Cohen Sons & Co in January 1951.

Stephenson No 3070 as PLA No 10 photographed at Custom House shed in 1934. (Author's Collection)

The Victoria and Albert Docks

London & India Docks Company Royal Docks 0-6-0ST Stephenson No 3050

Name: (*Looe*)

Manufacturer: Robert Stephenson & Co Ltd

Built: 26th April 1901

Works number: 3050

Running number: No 11 (L&ID Co and PLA)

At the Docks: 1901–1950

The second "new" Stephenson engine to arrive at the Royal Docks under the L&ID Co was not exactly pristine. No 3050 named *Looe* had been dispatched ex-works to the Liskeard & Looe Railway in Cornwall but was found unsuitable for some of the gradients on that line. After only a few months, the loco was delivered by sea to London Docks, where it joined others from this maker at Custom House, arriving in green livery aboard the steamship *Brighton Harry*. No 3050 had minor differences to the others and a shorter saddle tank which reduced its water capacity to around 650 gallons but was otherwise very similar to its sisters. The loco reportedly was used occasionally on the Royal Albert Dock Passenger Railway and appears to have retained its name throughout its time with the Dock Company. Under the PLA it underwent a rebuild in 1914 and again in 1923 by Harland & Wolff when it was fitted with a new firebox. It moved to the Millwall Docks on 18th September 1943 after which its days ended there when withdrawn in 1949 and scrapped by George Cohen Sons & Co in December 1950.

The "second hand" Stephenson No 3050 as PLA No 11 photographed at Victoria Docks on 1st September 1935. (H.C. Casserley)

London & India Docks Company Royal Docks 0-6-0ST Stephenson No 3094

Manufacturer: Robert Stephenson & Co Ltd

Built: 14th August 1902

Works number: 3094

Running number: No 12 (L&ID Co and PLA)

At the Docks: 1902–1931

The third Stephenson loco to arrive at the Royal Docks under the ownership of the London & India Dock Co was No 3094, sent new from their Newcastle works. It was rebuilt by the PLA in 1919 and, for while, spent some time at Tilbury during the 1920s, afterwards remaining in dock service at the Royals until laid aside in 1930. Around April the following year it was purchased by dealers George Cohen Sons & Co in 1931 who, in turn, sold the loco on to the firm of Fountain & Burnley Ltd at their North Gawber Colliery in West Yorkshire. It was finally scrapped there by the firm of William Hardman in June 1958.

Stephenson No 3094 pictured, minus its coupling rods, outside Newcastle Central Station on 14th August 1902 awaiting transportation to the London & India Dock Co where it ran as their No 12. (Stephenson Locomotive Society)

Locomotives purchased by the London & India Docks Company at Royal Docks

Maker	Works No	Name	Type	Running No	Date Arrived	PLA Number	Date Departed	Notes
RS	3070		0-6-0ST	10	1901	10	1951	Sold for scrap
RS	3050	*Looe*	0-6-0ST	11	1901	11	1950	Sold for scrap
RS	3094		0-6-0ST	12	1902	12	1931	Sold

CHAPTER 3

The Royal Docks

Upon its £23,000,000 acquisition of the former independent docks on 31st March 1909, the Port of London Authority set about its task of renewing both the docks infrastructure and its railways. Its priority was the rebuilding of the quaysides and their equipment and a total of £12,000,000 was allocated for these works, but more expenditure was needed on the dilapidated tracks and locomotives that coordinated the movement of goods around the estates and prepared them for onward transit over the nation's main lines.

The largest concentration of former Dock Company locomotives was at the Royal Victoria and Royal Albert Docks where twenty engines were stationed at Custom House. These were Dubs 1438–1441 (PLA numbers 1–4), Stephenson numbers 2844, 2845, 2981, 2982, 2983, 3050, 3070 and 3094 (5–12), Fox Walker numbers 149, 288 and 263 (11A, 12A and 13), Yorkshire Engine No 284 (14), unnumbered Falcon (15), Manning Wardle No 905 (16), unnumbered Ruston Proctor (18) Hunslet No 343 (19). FW No 288 was soon sent off to the West India Docks in 1911 where it ended its working days a year later.

Over the period 1910–1911 the four Dubs engines had their cabs rebuilt more substantially. They were now totally enclosed although a couple of the locos had a canvas back sheet at the rear. When they emerged from the workshops they had all been painted in the brick red livery that had been adopted by the PLA from its L&ID Co predecessors. The authority later experimented with a red-brown or chocolate colour with black bands and yellow lining but that gave way to royal blue from around 1920.

In 1911 a contract for a new pumping station at the Gallions entrance to the Royal Albert Dock saw the employment of the Falcon engine (PLA No 15) during the works. This being a precursor to the major works of building the dock extension (the King George V Dock) which began the following year.

The PLA began its replacements of stock, initially by hiring Stratford based locos from the Great Eastern Railway but it was not until 1911 that the first new engines arrived, these were three 0-6-0 tanks built by Andrew Barclay. Numbers 1236 and 1237 arrived that year at a cost of £1287 each, while the third, No 1238, went to Tilbury. All were delivered in the standard red livery.

The trio were originally supplied with rear bunkers but this proved unsatisfactory and they were almost immediately returned to the makers for modification to side bunkers. Their principal dimensions were:

Cylinders: 16in x 24in
Driving Wheels: 3ft 9in
Boiler Pressure: 160psi
Wheelbase: 9ft 6in
Water Capacity: 900gals
Coal Capacity: 25cwt
Weight: 36ton 0cwt

A further three, numbers 1294, 1300 and 1301 (PLA numbers 41, 42 and 43), arrived in the following year, by which time the price had risen to £1342 each, while a seventh, No 1302, appeared in 1913. All had been painted blue by the mid-1920s apart from the last one which, as PLA No 44, had the distinction of carrying its red livery throughout its entire time at the docks. The later examples also had a slight alteration to their cab sides and the rear windows were changed from round to square. All had their centre wheel flanges removed, this being a feature with six coupled PLA locos to best negotiate the sharp curves of the dock lines. The Great Eastern Railway continued to provide locos in times of shortage and a variety of classes were sent to Custom House, among those noted were numbers 262, 303, 415 and 416.

The new influx of Barclays still left the PLA short of motive power and, in 1913, six new 0-6-0T engines were ordered from the Hohenzollern Locomotive Works at Dusseldorf, the firm being chosen for its competitive prices. The PLA board was equally divided over the deal and the chairman cast his deciding vote in favour of the contract but by the time the locos had been completed the First World War had broken out and they were never delivered. In their place, six more 0-6-0T engines were ordered, this time from makers Hudswell Clarke who delivered them in 1915 at a cost of £1865 each. Three of these, numbers 1153, 1154 and 1155 (PLA numbers 50, 51 and 52) came to the Royal Docks and the other trio numbers 1101, 1102 and 1103 (45, 46 and 49) were allocated to Tilbury.

The design of these HC engines was so successful it was adapted as the standard model for many more orders and by the end of WWI another six had been purchased for the Royal Docks, these being numbers 1244, 1245, 1254, 1255, 1323 and 1324 (PLA numbers 58–63). Two more, numbers 1414 and 1415 (64 and 65), arrived in 1920 and were the first to arrive painted in the new PLA blue livery. Their principal dimensions were:

Cylinders:	16in x 24in
Driving Wheels:	3ft 9in
Boiler Pressure:	160psi
Wheelbase:	10ft 0in
Water capacity:	1200gals
Weight:	42ton 0cwt

In the meantime, something of a clear-out of the remaining old dock company locos had begun with another 12 engines being either sold or scrapped by 1920. The first casualty had been Hunslet No 343, scrapped in 1910, followed by the Ruston Proctor, sold in 1912. While passing the tobacco warehouse in Victoria Docks in late 1912, FW No 149 suffered an explosion which removed its dome cover, safety valves and part of its cab. The injuries to its crew are not recorded but the loco was sold to George Cohen Sons & Co as scrap the following year. Sister engine FW No 288 had ended its days at the West India Docks where it sat outside the South Dock shed with condemned locos *Swift* (JF No 3807) and *Bee* (HE No 235) until disposed of in 1913.

Next to go was the Falcon loco, sold in 1914, followed by YE 284 (sold) and FW 263 (scrapped), both in 1917. Dubs No 1439 was loaned to the West India Docks during WWI but by 1915 the Dubs quartet were worn out. Replacement engines were sought using expenditure withheld on their repairs and the foursome were laid up in 1917 but held in reserve for emergency use or spares until finally disposed of in 1920, while MW 905 was also in sold in 1920. During this period MW No 1008 was brought over from Millwall in 1917 to assist in the war effort and by 1920 the roll call at Custom House in PLA order was:

No 5   RS No 2844
No 6   RS No 2845
No 7   RS No 2981
No 9   RS No 2983
No 10 RS No 3070
No 11 RS No 3050
No 12 RS No 3094
No 34 MW No 1008
No 38 AB No 1236
No 39 AB No 1237
No 41 AB No 1294
No 42 AB No 1300
No 43 AB No 1301
No 44 AB No 1302
No 50 HC No 1153
No 51 HC No 1154
No 52 HC No 1155
No 58 HC No 1244
No 59 HC No 1245
No 60 HC No 1254
No 61 HC No 1255
No 62 HC No 1323
No 63 HC No 1324
No 64 HC No 1414
No 65 HC No 1415

During the First World War a warehouse at the eastern end of the Royal Albert Dock was being used as a store for an Artillery Company with a rail link running thorough a cutting to the docks sidings. During the course of shunting supplies there, Barclay No 1237 (PLA No 39) and RS 2844 (No 5) entered the cutting from opposite ends and collided. No 39 left the rails and embedded its front end in the bank and this resulted in a shallower rectangular buffer beam being fitted as a replacement for the original.

PLA Royal Docks 0-6-0T Barclay No 1236

Manufacturer:	Andrew Barclay Sons & Co Ltd
Built:	12th March 1911
Works number:	1236
Running number:	No 38
At the Docks:	1911– 1941 and 1945–1951

Dispatched new to the PLA at Custom House, Barclay No 1236 worked in the Royal Docks until transferred on loan to the Mersey Docks & Harbour Board in January 1941. After its wartime spell there it returned in November 1945 before moving to Tilbury Docks in July 1946. It remained there during the post war years and after some period of storage was cut up, along with sister AB No 1237 around the end of 1951.

The Royal Docks

PLA Royal Docks 0-6-0T Barclay No 1237

Manufacturer: Andrew Barclay Sons & Co Ltd
Built: 22nd March 1911
Works number: 1237
Running number: No 39
At the Docks: 1911–1940 and 1946–1951

New from the makers, Barclay No 1237 worked the quays at the Royal Docks until the war effort saw it loaned to the Manchester Ship Canal in August 1940 where it worked mostly at Salford Docks. After returning to London in January 1946 it was transferred to Tilbury Docks on 1st July that year where it was badly damaged in a collision with AB No 1302 (PLA No 44), but remained working there until scrapped with AB No 1236 around 1951.

Barclay No 1237 as PLA No 39 parked at the Royal Victoria Docks on 1st September 1934. (H C Casserley)

The first new PLA loco was Barclay No 1236 in 1911, seen here at Custom House as No 38 after the removal of its rear bunker. (John Alsop Collection)

PLA Royal Docks 0-6-0T Barclay No 1294

Manufacturer:	Andrew Barclay Sons & Co Ltd
Built:	30th July 1912
Works number:	1294
Running number:	No 41
At the Docks:	1912–1946

Four more locos arrived from Barclay in 1912. The first, No 1294, was sent new to the Royal Docks but was soon transferred for duties at the West India Docks and based at Millwall before returning to the Royals on 2nd May 1934, where, having worked through the war years, it was sold for scrap to A R Wright for £70 in February 1946.

PLA Royal Docks 0-6-0T Barclay No 1300

Name:	*(Palma)*
Manufacturer:	Andrew Barclay Sons & Co Ltd
Built:	13th September 1912
Works number:	1300
Running number:	No 42
At the Docks:	1912–1940 and 1946–1948

The second of four Barclays sent new to the Custom House in 1912, No 1300 saw service at the Royal Docks before the Second World War saw it loaned to Ellesmere Port on the Manchester Ship Canal in July 1940, remaining there until its return to London in February 1946. However, its second spell was short lived as it was withdrawn in August 1946 and sold to the Aberthaw & Bristol Channel Portland Cement Company Ltd at Rhoose, South Glamorgan in 1948. While there, it retained its PLA No 42 and was named *Palma* (the letters A and M being inserted into PLA) and gave many more years service before being sold to scrap merchant John Cashmore at Newport Gwent in 1964.

PLA Royal Docks 0-6-0T Barclay No 1301

Manufacturer:	Andrew Barclay Sons & Co Ltd
Built:	21st September 1912
Works number:	1301
Running number:	No 43
At the Docks:	1912–1948

The third of four Barclay engines supplied new to the PLA in 1912. This one, No 1301 saw its time at the docks ended after the Second World War when, following withdrawal in July 1946 and, after a period of dereliction, it was sold to T Hall & Sons at Llansamlet, West Glamorgan in 1948 and moved on to the National Coal Board's Silverwood Colliery in Yorkshire in the same year. After a decade in the coal industry it was sold for scrap to F Tingle of Kilnhurst, South Yorkshire.

The Royal Docks

Barclay No 1294 (PLA No 41) spent time at the India & Millwall Docks where it was one of the earlier successful 0-6-0 locos to move to the Millwall shed. It is pictured there, still in its original red livery, with attendant crew and shed personnel in the early 1930s. (Frank Jones Collection/Industrial Locomotive Society)

Barclay No 1300 as PLA No 42 stands outside Custom House Shed. Its service continued for many years in South Wales after leaving the docks. (R K Blencowe Collection)

Barclay No 1301 stands idle at the Victoria Docks on 1st September 1934. (H C Casserley)

PLA Royal Docks 0-6-0T Barclay No 1302

Manufacturer:	Andrew Barclay Sons & Co Ltd
Built:	21st September 1912
Works number:	1302
Running number:	No 44
At the Docks:	1912–1953

The last of a quartet of Barclays sent to the PLA in 1912. This one, No 1302 left the works with No 1301 and joined its sisters at Custom House. Its years at the Royal Docks came to an end when transferred to Tilbury on 18th May 1944 where it later suffered damage in a collision with sister AB No 1237 and, after seeing out the war years, it continued there until sold for scrap to George Cohen, Sons & Co Ltd in 1953.

PLA Royal Docks 0-6-0T Hudswell Clarke No 1153

Manufacturer:	Hudswell, Clarke & Co Ltd
Built:	20th September 1915
Works number:	1153
Running number:	No 50
At the Docks:	1915–1940 and 1946–1947

One of an initial trio supplied new to Custom House during The Great War, No 1153 was rebuilt in 1925 and was one of several locomotives dispatched to other ports during the second conflict, being sent on loan to Ellesmere Port on the Manchester Ship Canal in April 1940. It returned in March 1946 but was in such poor condition it was cannibalised for spares in 1947 with the remains being broken up the following year.

PLA Royal Docks 0-6-0T Hudswell Clarke No 1154

Manufacturer:	Hudswell, Clarke & Co Ltd
Built:	27th September 1915
Works number:	1154
Running number:	No 51
At the Docks:	1915–1940 and 1945–1960

The second of three HCs purchased in 1915 for work in the Royal Docks. No 1154 was, like others, sent on loan to the Manchester Ship Canal for service there in the Second World War spending some time at Partington. Having left in August 1940 it returned to Custom House in 1945 before being transferred to Tilbury on 3rd October 1947. After overhaul there in 1953 it was back at the Royals on 28th May 1955. By October 1957 it had been fitted with steam heating apparatus for banana train working until laid aside in 1959, and being scrapped the following year when it was sold to Mayer, Newman & Co for £530.

The Royal Docks

Barclay No 1302 pictured at the Victoria Docks with RS 3050 on 1st September 1934. (H C Casserley)

Hudswell Clarke No 1153 pictured near Custom House Station possibly in the 1920s during its first spell at the Royal Docks. (Frank Jones Collection/Industrial Locomotive Society)

A rain streaked Hudswell Clarke No 1154 on duty at Custom House on 18th October 1958. (Frank Jones Collection/Industrial Locomotive Society)

PLA Royal Docks 0-6-0T Hudswell Clarke No 1155

Manufacturer:	Hudswell, Clarke & Co Ltd
Built:	30th September 1915
Works number:	1155
Running number:	No 52
At the Docks:	1915–1940 and 1945–1956

The last of three HC locos purchased by the PLA for work at the Royal Docks in 1915. As with the other two, No 1155 was sent to the Manchester Ship Canal for wartime service at Partington with HC No 1154, leaving in November 1940 and returning in December 1945. After being rebuilt with parts from HC No 1153 its peacetime duties at Custom House lasted for just over a decade when it was cannibalised for spares in 1956, the rest being sold as scrap to the firm of I Bier for £47 10s in 1956, although several dismembered remains were still evident on 12th October 1957.

PLA Royal Docks 0-6-0T Hudswell, Clarke No 1244

Manufacturer:	Hudswell, Clarke & Co Ltd
Built:	23rd April 1917
Works number:	1244
Running number:	No 58
At the Docks:	1917–1960

After a two year lull in PLA arrivals from Hudswell Clarke, supplies resumed when No 1244 was sent to Custom House at the Royal Docks in 1917. After a decade of service the loco was rebuilt in 1927 and later transferred to Tilbury Docks with No 1414 on 5th June 1944 to assist in the war effort. It remained there and underwent repairs in 1957 before being sent back to the Royals in 1958 where, after two more years, it was scrapped in 1960 when sold, along with No 1154, to Mayer Newman & Co for £530.

PLA Royal Docks 0-6-0T Hudswell Clarke No 1245

Manufacturer:	Hudswell, Clarke & Co Ltd
Built:	3rd May 1917
Works number:	1245
Running number:	No 59
At the Docks:	1917–1960

The second of four Hudswell Clarke 0-6-0 tanks delivered to Custom House in 1917 was No 1245, being ex-works that year. As PLA No 59 it remained in the Royal Docks until sent to Tilbury during the Second World War, then returning to the Royals in January 1956. Its end came when sold to the firm of Meyer, Newman & Co for £530 and scrapped in 1960.

The Royal Docks

Hudswell Clarke No 1155 passes the Missions to Seaman Hostel at Custom House on 12th June 1954. (L S Freeman/ Transport Treasury)

HC No 1244 as PLA No 58 in its Tilbury days, photographed at the shed on 12th May 1947, still adorned with its wartime blackout markings. (H C Casserley)

Vintage vehicles accompany Hudswell Clarke No 1245 and the vessel "Balantia" at the King George V Dock on 25th September 1957. (R C Riley/Transport Treasury)

PLA Royal Docks 0-6-0T Hudswell Clarke No 1254

Manufacturer: Hudswell, Clarke & Co Ltd
Built: 25th June 1917
Works number: 1254
Running number: No 60
At the Docks: 1917–1960

The third of four Hudswell Clarke engines delivered to the Royal Docks in 1917. No 1254 left the makers that year and later spent time at Tilbury. Having returned to Custom House on 4th January 1942 for heavy repairs it made a second visit to Tilbury on 24th March 1944, joining others that were sent there during the war effort for the second conflict, this time staying until a return to the Royal Docks in June 1956, where, four years later it was sold to Meyer, Newman & Co for £530 and scrapped in 1960.

PLA Royal Docks 0-6-0T Hudswell Clarke No 1255

Manufacturer: Hudswell, Clarke & Co Ltd
Built: 27th July 1917
Works number: 1255
Running number: No 61 (PLA), 18 (Bowes) and 29 (NCB)
At the Docks: 1917–1941 and 1945–1947

The final Hudswell Clarke to arrive at the Royal Docks in 1917 was No 1255. Like several other Custom House locos it was rebuilt in 1927 and remained allocated there until early in World War Two when it was dispatched, along with Barclay No 1236, to the Mersey Docks & Harbour Board in January 1941. After hostilities had ended the pair returned to Custom House in November 1945 but No 61 saw only a short spell "back home" before being disposed of. Having undergone an overhaul at its makers from April 1947 it was sold in 1948 to the National Coal Board's Bowes Railway, County Durham, in November that year. Based at the Springwell Bank Foot loco shed, Wardley it ran as Bowes No 18 and then NCB No 29. After repairs by Locomotive builders W G Bagnall of Stafford it was renumbered as works 6399 by them. In October 1961 it spent a further spell away for repairs, this time at Andrew Barclay's works in Kilmarnock and was back by July the following year. A transfer to Derwenthaugh loco shed at Swalwell came in October 1963 and there it was eventually scrapped on site by D. Sep. Bowran in April 1966.

PLA Royal Docks 0-6-0T Hudswell Clarke No 1323

Manufacturer: Hudswell, Clarke & Co Ltd
Built: 24th April 1918
Works number: 1323
Running number: No 62
At the Docks: 1918–1941 and 1946–1960

The final year of the First World War saw two more Hudswell Clarke locos arrive at the Royal Docks. No 1323 was sent from the makers in April that year (the other was No 1324 a few months later). As PLA No 62 it was based at Custom House until being sent to the Port of Bristol Authority at Avonmouth Docks in November 1940, remaining there throughout the war years until returning to London in January 1946. Back at the Royal Docks it gave several more years of service until sold to Meyer, Newman & Co for £530 and scrapped in 1960.

The Royal Docks

Hudswell Clarke No 1254 in its early days as PLA No 60 pictured at Tilbury Docks. (Author's Collection)

Hudswell Clarke No 1255 displays PLA No 61 in both plate and painted form at Custom House, possibly after its return from wartime service in Liverpool. (Frank Jones Collection/Industrial Locomotive Society)

A grimy Hudswell Clarke No 1323 is paired with sister No 1455 awaiting boiler washout at Custom House. (Frank Jones Collection/Industrial Locomotive Society)

PLA Royal Docks 0-6-0T Hudswell Clarke No 1324

Manufacturer:	Hudswell, Clarke & Co Ltd
Built:	14th October 1918
Works number:	1324
Running number:	No 63
At the Docks:	1918–1940 and 1946–1959

The second of two Hudswell Clarke locos built for the PLA in 1918. This one, No 1324 was sent to Custom House in October. Having been rebuilt in 1926 it joined the exodus of PLA locos on loan to the Manchester Ship Canal in July 1940 and worked mainly at Salford Docks. After returning to the Royal Docks in April 1946 it was transferred to Millwall Docks in October 1947, spending two years there before coming back to Custom House in November 1949. A further eight years of service followed before it was withdrawn in November 1957 and finally scrapped by George Cohen Sons & Co Ltd in October 1959.

PLA Royal Docks 0-6-0T Hudswell Clarke No 1414

Manufacturer:	Hudswell, Clarke & Co Ltd
Built:	5th November 1920
Works number:	1414
Running number:	No 64
At the Docks:	1920–1953

The first new arrival at the PLA in 1920 was Hudswell Clarke No 1414. It underwent a rebuild in 1927 and remained at Custom House until transferred to Tilbury on 5th June 1944 with HC No 1244. The records state it returned to the Royal Docks in January 1946 but it was photographed at Tilbury in May the following year. Its end came when scrapped in 1953 by George Cohen Sons & Co Ltd.

PLA Royal Docks 0-6-0T Hudswell Clarke No 1415

Manufacturer:	Hudswell, Clarke & Co Ltd
Built:	25th November 1920
Works number:	1415
Running number:	No 65
At the Docks:	1920–1960

The second 1920 arrival at Custom House from Hudswell Clarke was No 1415. As PLA No 65 it underwent a rebuild in 1926 and worked its whole life at the Royal Docks before being sold for scrap to Cox & Danks at Bromley by Bow for £450 on 30th April 1960 and was broken up in the following month.

The Royal Docks

Hudswell Clarke No 1324 in a sorry state minus its chimney and coupling rods after withdrawal and being stored at Custom House on 4th April 1959. (L S Freeman/Transport Treasury)

Hudswell Clarke No 1414 pictured at Tilbury Docks. Officially, it returned to the Royal Docks in 1946 but this photo is dated 17th May 1947. Note the wartime blackout markings still evident along its frame. (H C Casserley)

Hudswell Clarke No 1415 poses for the camera as PLA No 65 at Custom House. (Frank Jones Collection/ Industrial Locomotive Society)

39

London's Dock Railways: The Royal Docks, North Woolwich and Silvertown

During the First World War the PLA was offered a free trial of a battery electric locomotive in 1916 but, owing to the war, the experiment was delayed until the peacetime of 1919. The experiment took place at the Royal Victoria Docks flour mills of Joseph Rank Ltd with a loco that was supplied by Hugh Wood & Co of Gateshead. This was a four-wheeled engine built by the American firm of Jeffrey Manufacturing Company. The quoted price of the engine was £2,200 but the general docks traffic proved too much for the loco which was reportedly then sold to Mather & Platt Ltd in Manchester.

With the increasing size of shipping outgrowing the existing facilities, the PLA commenced extending the Royal Docks. Original plans included new docks both north and south of the Albert Dock but the northern basin at Beckton was never built, while the other, to the south of the Albert Dock, was commenced in 1912. At first referred to as the Albert Dock Extension, the contract was awarded to S Pearson & Son Ltd, but the intervention of war had slowed progress and, after the hostilities were over, the PLA assumed direct control of the project using Pearson's plant and locomotives of which there were 17 employed. Upon completion, the new dock was officially opened on 8th July 1921 by His Majesty King George V, after whom the dock was named. It had three miles of quays and covered 64 acres, and could accommodate vessels of 30,000 tons. It also contained London's largest drydock.

The Royal Docks as a whole then covered over 11,000 acres with 12.75 miles of quays and its 246 acres of enclosed docks represented the world's largest area of impounded water. This was the last major dock construction project at London although there were other significant improvement schemes to both the India and Millwall docks and to those at Tilbury.

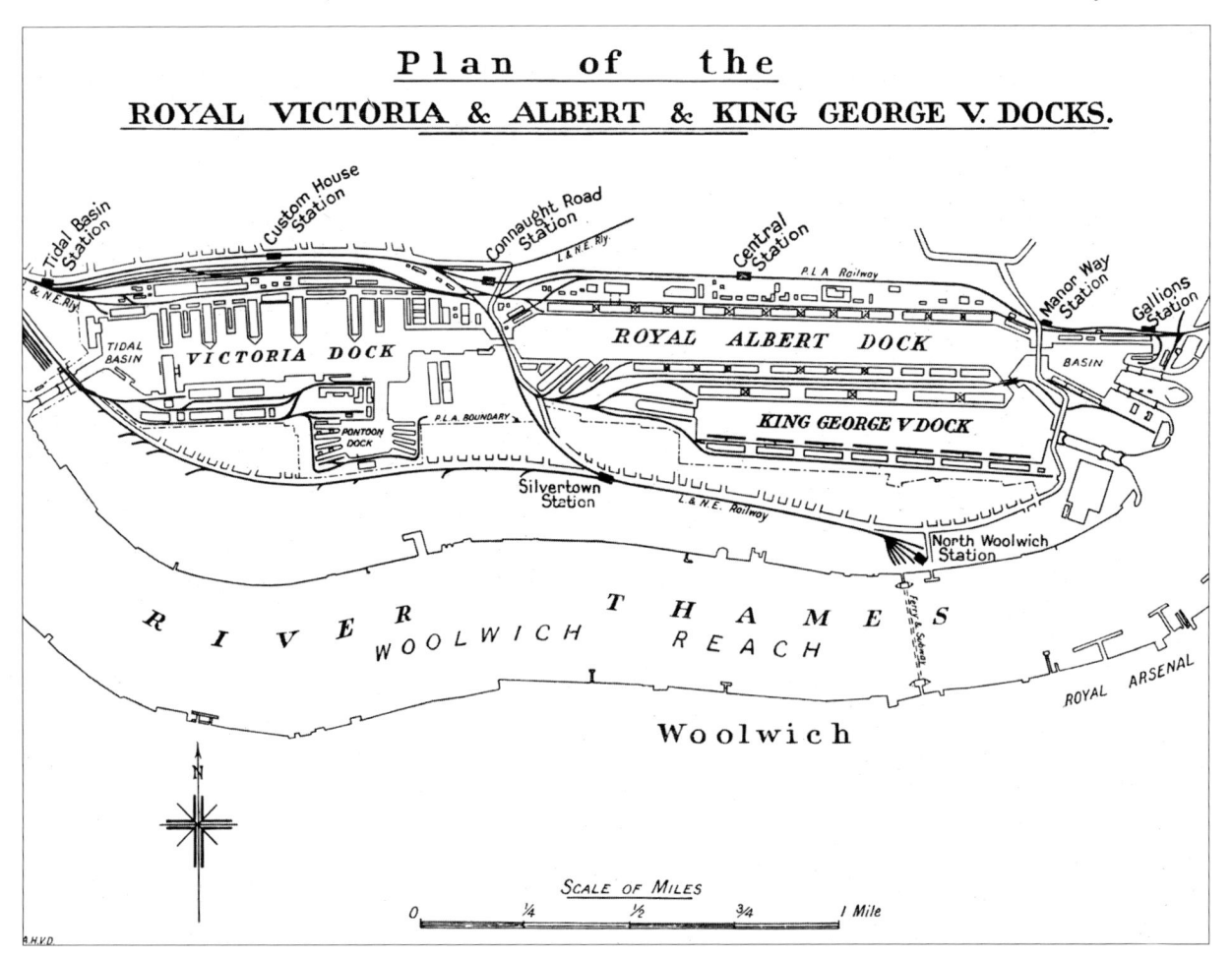

The railways in and around the Royal Docks in the 1920s. (Author's Collection)

40

The Royal Docks

Repairs to locos and rolling stock had been carried out by the PLA themselves but, from 1921, all marine and mechanical engineering was outsourced to Harland & Wolff Ltd who occupied the maintenance works adjacent to the Custom House running shed and also leased a dozen sites across the entire PLA system.

About this time, RS No 3094 (PLA No 12) became the first Custom House loco to don the new blue livery. With its PLA plates having been removed, it was fully lettered and numbered and, possibly to mark the occasion of the new dock opening, it had the PLA's coat of arms embellished on its cab sides. Unfortunately, this grandeur was quickly deflated when soon after leaving the shops it fell foul of some points and ended up on its side. The embarrassment was completed when protocol decreed that the heraldry should be painted over and it was afterwards sent to Tilbury for a spell in the 1920s.

Stephenson No 3050 *Looe* was also prone to mishaps. In one incident it ran "full tilt" into the closed shed doors while, on another occasion, it showered its attendant shunters with hot water and ashes as they rode along on it. A more serious accident occurred when it ran down the gradient at Custom House and became derailed with a train of meat wagons across the main exchange sidings. In doing so it held up dock operations for many hours. On 30th April 1929 RS No 2844 was sent to the India Docks for duties on the banana trade before returning to Custom House where it spent much of its time laying idle.

At first the PLA had carried on the tradition of the old dock companies in fixing number plates to its locomotives, generally an oval shape with the running number at the centre and the letters PLA and the date above and below it. After the new blue livery came into being, the letters and numbers were merely painted in white on the tank and cab sides while the number was repeated in yellow on the buffer beams but even the style and size of the lettering differed from time to time. In some cases the PLA plate remained in place, together with the painted identity.

The blue PLA livery was introduced gradually at each dock, but many of the older engines never received it. Although basically royal blue with white lining, there were several versions which varied from dock to dock, and even changed over different periods at the same locations. The main variations were:
1. Two white lines enclosing a black band.
2. Two white lines with a broader black band around the edges of tanks.
3. As 1 but with a third white line on the outside (this version was only used at Tilbury).

In the post war austerity years the shade of blue varied greatly (depending on what paint was available) and quite often the lining was left off altogether. In fact, during that time, the hard worked locos suffered a lack of maintenance and, with a coating of grime, their livery was often described as "dirt colour".

The Port of London Authority coat of arms. Its celebratory application to the cab sides of loco No 12 was deemed "unethical". (Author's Collection)

41

London's Dock Railways: The Royal Docks, North Woolwich and Silvertown

The opening of the King George V Dock saw the influx of six more new locomotives, of the now standard Hudswell Clarke design, arrive between 1921 and 1927. These were numbers 1453, 1454, 1455, 1596, 1597 and 1598 (the latter pair costing £2475 each) and, after the frenzy of locomotive purchases through the 1920s, that completed the restocking for the time being, although, during this period, they were joined by MW 1106 on transfer from Millwall in 1923 and the 1920s complement at Custom House became:

No 5   RS No 2844
No 6   RS No 2845
No 7   RS No 2981
No 9   RS No 2983
No 10 RS No 3070
No 11 RS No 3050
No 12 RS No 3094
No 34 MW No 1008
No 35 MW No 1106
No 38 AB No 1236
No 39 AB No 1237
No 41 AB No 1294
No 42 AB No 1300
No 43 AB No 1301
No 44 AB No 1302
No 50 HC No 1153
No 51 HC No 1154
No 52 HC No 1155
No 58 HC No 1244
No 59 HC No 1245
No 60 HC No 1254
No 61 HC No 1255
No 62 HC No 1323
No 63 HC No 1324
No 64 HC No 1414
No 65 HC No 1415
No 66 HC No 1453
No 67 HC No 1454
No 68 HC No 1455
No 71 HC No 1596
No 72 HC No 1597
No 73 HC No 1598

Of these, Manning Wardles, numbers 1106 and 1008, were sold in 1926 and 1927 respectively, while the older Stephenson locos were disposed of as follows. No 2845 was scrapped in 1926, No 2983 sold for scrap in 1926, No 2981 sold for scrap in 1929, No 3094 sold in 1931 and No 2844 sold in 1937. The remainder were all in service at the outbreak of World War Two.

A hive of activity on the quayside at the Royal Albert Docks in the 1920s. (Author's Collection)

The Royal Docks

In the 1930s the PLA had a total of 602 wagons for internal use of which 273 were open trucks, 76 were box vans and 77 insulated vans. There were also 176 flat trolleys that were used for the internal movement of timber, mainly at the Millwall Docks, which handled a third of the UK's imports at that time. There were also over 100 freight and passenger trains daily and in 1934 alone some 1,155,685 tons of goods were carried by the PLA railways by means of 429,887 wagon movements.

The growing size of ships required large scale improvements to the Royal Docks and works began in 1935 to deepen and widen quays, and also to increase the size of the Connaught Cutting. The Victoria Dock had seen little improvement since its building and the now crumbling original five finger jetties were removed while the north quay was rebuilt with large modern warehouses and greater rail access.

Old style plates similar to those of the former dock companies were adopted by the PLA but gave way to painted numbers and lettering from the 1920s when the new liveries were applied. (H C Casserley)

The interior of the Royal Victoria Docks meat shed at Tidal Basin where hanging chains transported sides of beef and sheep carcases from ships to cold stores and onward transit. (Author's Collection)

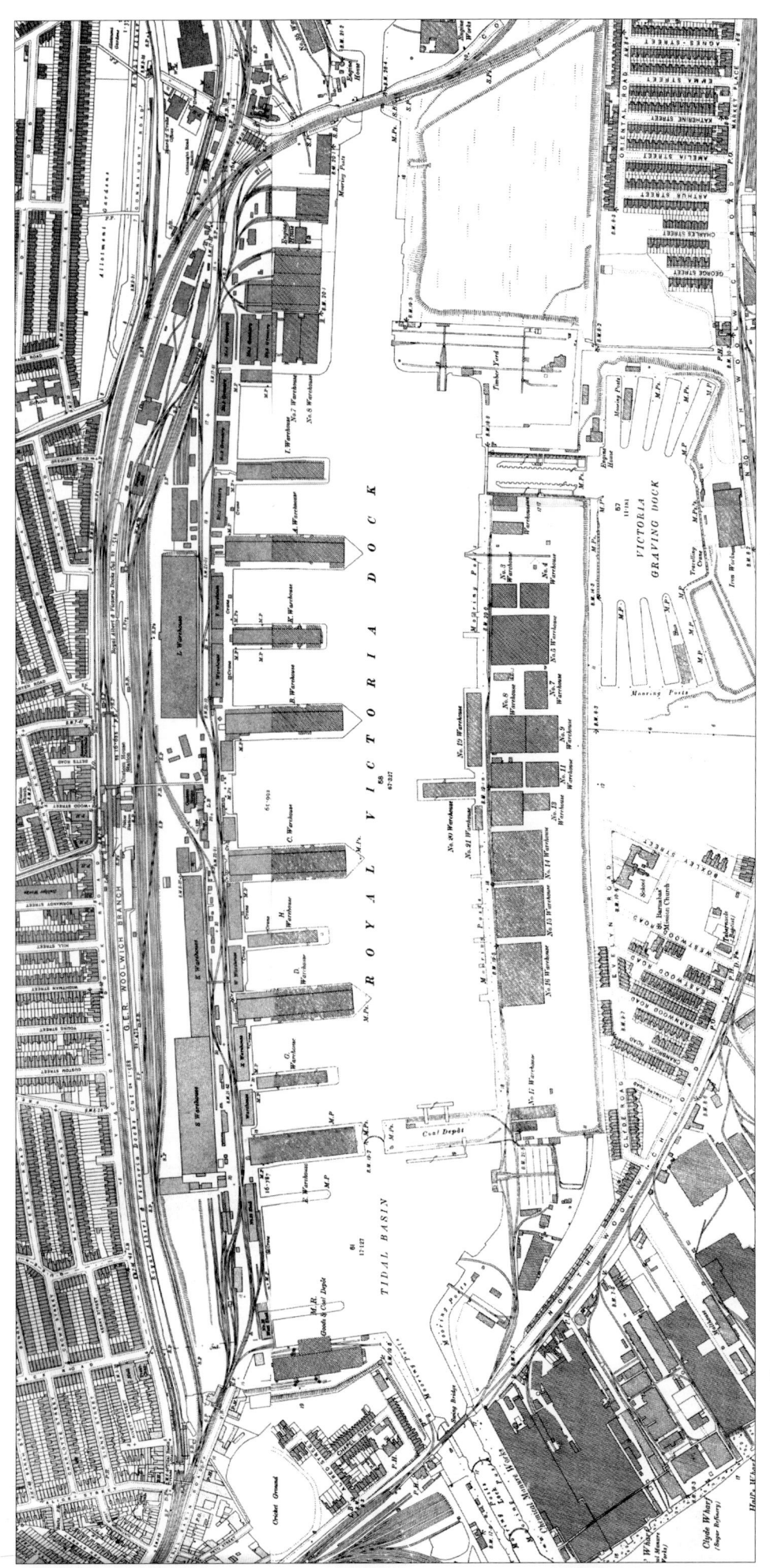

At the turn of the 20th century the Royal Victoria Dock still had its original finger jetties along the northern quay. These were removed in the rebuilding of the dock in the 1930s. (Crown Copyright)

The Royal Docks

PLA Royal Docks 0-6-0T Hudswell Clarke No 1453

Manufacturer:	Hudswell, Clarke & Co Ltd
Built:	20th December 1921
Works number:	1453
Running number:	No 66
At the Docks:	1921–1960

The first new arrival at the Royal Docks in 1921 was Hudswell Clarke No 1453 sent from the makers along with sisters 1454 and 1455. As PLA No 66 it appears to have led a fairly uneventful existence based at Custom House until it was sent for scrap to the Bromley by Bow firm of Cox & Danks Ltd for £450 on 30th April 1960 and broken up in the following month.

Hudswell Clarke No 1453 cruises past austerity Hunslet No 2414 (PLA No 79) and a line of sister engines at Custom House depot on 14th March 1958. (Alec Swain/Transport Treasury)

PLA Royal Docks 0-6-0T Hudswell Clarke No 1454

Manufacturer:	Hudswell, Clarke & Co Ltd
Built:	1921
Works number:	1454
Running number:	No 67 (No 73 from 1960)
At the Docks:	1921–1963

This was the second of a trio of Hudswell Clarke locos dispatched to the Royal Docks along with numbers 1453 and 1455. Having been rebuilt in 1928 it was transferred to Tilbury on 13th May 1944 during the build up to D-Day, returning to Custom House in January 1946. It suffered a change of identity when renumbered by the PLA from 67 to 73 in 1960 after HC No 1598 was disposed of but its new guise lasted only until around April 1963 when sold for scrap to the firm of Cox & Danks at Bromley by Bow. (This loco is illustrated on page 47.)

PLA Royal Docks 0-6-0T Hudswell Clarke No 1455

Manufacturer:	Hudswell, Clarke & Co Ltd
Built:	29th December 1921
Works number:	1455
Running number:	No 68
At the Docks:	1921–1960

Last of a Hudswell Clarke trio dispatched to Custom House at the end of 1921, the others being numbers 1453 and 1454. After almost 40 years service it joined several other locos at the Bromley by Bow premises of scrap merchants Cox & Danks on 30th April 1960, having been sold for £450 and being broken up in the following month.

PLA Royal Docks 0-6-0T Hudswell Clarke No 1596

Manufacturer:	Hudswell, Clarke & Co Ltd
Built:	23rd July 1927
Works number:	1596
Running number:	No 71
At the Docks:	1927–1959

The first new arrival in over five years at Custom House, Hudswell Clarke No 1596 served all its time at the Royal Docks before being withdrawn in September 1956 and later scrapped on site by George Cohen Sons & Co Ltd in October 1959.

PLA Royal Docks 0-6-0T Hudswell Clarke No 1597

Manufacturer:	Hudswell, Clarke & Co Ltd
Built:	29th August 1927
Works number:	1597
Running number:	No 72
At the Docks:	1927–1961

Sent from the makers works on the 29th August 1927 Hudswell Clarke No 1597 began an uneventful time at Custom House, stabled there throughout is entire working life until scrapped around 1961.

The Royal Docks

Hudswell Clarke No 1454 steams away at Custom House on 21st May 1955. A change of identity took place in 1960 when its PLA number changed from 67 to 73. (H C Casserley)

HC No 1596 as PLA No 71 pictured at the Custom House shed in 1934. (Author's Collection)

Hudswell Clarke No 1597 at the Royal Docks on 21st January 1961. (© 2010 - 53A Models of Hull Collection/R Munday)

PLA Royal Docks 0-6-0T Hudswell Clarke No 1598

Manufacturer: Hudswell, Clarke & Co Ltd
Built: 19th September 1927
Works number: 1598
Running number: No 73
At the Docks: 1927–1960

Another of the Hudswell Clarke arrivals in 1927 was No 1598. After its debut at Custom House it spent all its working life at the Royal Docks before being sold to the firm of Gomm & Searle Ltd for £375 and scrapped along with numerous others in 1960. Its PLA number was afterwards transferred to a rebuilt No 67 (HC No 1454).

Hudswell Clarke No 1598 pictured as new at the Royal Docks in 1927. (Author's Collection)

CHAPTER 4

War and Peace at the Royals

In 1940, with the fear of air raids upon the capital, a considerable amount of shipping was switched to ports in the north and west of the country, and the War Department, now in control of London's Docks, dispatched a number of the PLA's locos to those distant locations. Several went to the Manchester Ship Canal, Liverpool Docks and Avonmouth, remaining there until peacetime saw them return. Six Custom House locos went to the Manchester Ship Canal, they were AB numbers 1237 (PLA No 39) and 1300 (42) along with HC numbers 1153 (50), 1154 (51), 1155 (52) and 1324 (63), while AB No 1236 (38) and HC No 1255 (61) went to Liverpool and HC 1323 (62) was sent to Avonmouth. Two others were also sent away from Tilbury, but none from Millwall where RS No 3050 (11) was loaned from Custom House to assist during a loco shortage there in 1943 and RS No 3070 (10) followed it there to work in the West India Docks from 12th August 1944. Both these locos remained based at Millwall until disposed of in 1950 when the pair had almost completed their half centuries at the Docks. With the wartime blackout being enforced, steps were taken to increase the night-time visibility of the locos that remained at the docks. White panels were painted along the frames of the engines while the buffer beams were also painted white.

After the war ended, in many cases the engines returning from the far off locations were much worse for wear and, when home again, their condition was not helped by the fact they were no longer allocated to specific crews, so failed to receive the care and respect they had previously enjoyed. Several were either cannibalised for spares or broken up as beyond economic repair. After its return, HC No 1324 (63) was sent to Millwall in October 1947 where it remained for two years before returning to the Royals in November 1949.

During the latter stages of the second conflict a number of War Department locos appeared at the Royal Docks, destined to be shipped to France following the D-Day invasion but, as events transpired, they were not needed there. Several of these were loaned for dock duties during the war effort and, when peacetime arrived, they were transferred to PLA stock, possibly by way of restitution for some of the earlier commandeered engines that were scrapped soon after their return. Twelve of these were 0-6-0ST "Austerity" types, two others were Hudswell Clarke 0-6-0 tanks, similar to the others already employed but with a longer wheelbase of 11ft 0in. These were supplemented by two second-hand locos, Manning Wardle No 1568 and Peckett No 489, the latter pair going to the India and Millwall Docks.

The main dimensions of the "Austerity" locos were:

Cylinders: 18in x 26in
Driving Wheels: 4ft 3in
Boiler Pressure: 170psi
Water Capacity: 1200gals
Coal Capacity: 2ton 5cwt
Wheelbase: 11ft 0in
Weight: 48ton 4cwt

Also evident in the build up to D-Day, two American-built 0-6-0 tanks from the USA Transportation Corps were seen working at Custom House. These were Davenport numbers 2534 and 2547 that came on hire from the GWR, where they were already on loan. They assisted at the Royals from 6th July 1944 until sent over to France in November that year. Others of this type were also used when 1305 and 4375 (from June to September 1944) and 4385, 4398 and 6165 (from July to September 1944) appeared in the docks. These were presumably also shipped over to France. During this hectic period HC No 1454 (PLA No 67) was sent to help out at Tilbury on 13th May 1944 until a peacetime return in January 1946.

The ex-WD engines retained in the docks were given PLA numbers in 1946 with the characters applied in white paint on their existing black livery. They also had larger buffers fitted to improve shunting on sharp curves. In the post war years, six of the early PLA Barclay and Hudswell Clarke purchases had gone by 1948. The last of the old dock company engines went in late 1950 when the two old Stephensons, numbers 3050 and 3070, ended their working days at Millwall. The reorganisation and overhaul of locos was now complete and no more engines were to arrive before 1953/4, which saw the addition of just three more new HC steamers (No 1875 to Millwall and numbers 1873 and 1874 to Tilbury) and another on loan at Custom House (Peckett No 2025) before the PLA turned to diesel traction from 1956.

PLA Royal Docks 0-6-0T Hudswell Clarke No 1719

Manufacturer:	Hudswell, Clarke & Co Ltd
Built:	3rd February 1943
Works number:	1719
Running number:	No 76 (PLA), 70070 (War Department)
Cylinders:	16in x 24in
Driving Wheels:	3ft 9in
Boiler Pressure:	160psi
Wheelbase:	11ft 0in
Water capacity:	1200gals
Weight:	42ton 0cwt
At the Docks:	1943–1961

The Second World War saw several War Department locomotives drafted to the Royal Docks. Having rolled off the assembly line in 1943 Hudswell Clarke No 1719 arrived at Custom House in August that year. Its WD number was 70070 which, after purchase by the docks in May 1946, became PLA No 76 and remained so until the loco was sold to Meyer, Newman & Co and scrapped around 1961

PLA Royal Docks 0-6-0T Hudswell Clarke No 1720

Manufacturer:	Hudswell, Clarke & Co Ltd
Built:	23rd March 1943
Works number:	1720
Running number:	No 77 (PLA), 70071 (War Department)
Dimensions:	As No 1719
At the Docks:	1943–1960

Another of the War Department Hudswell Clarke engines. This one, when new as WD No 70071, was originally based at Bicester in Oxfordshire and sent on loan to Custom House in July 1943. Having been purchased by the PLA in May 1946 and renumbered as their No 77 it lasted there until disposed of in 1960 when sold as scrap to Meyer, Newman & Co for £530.

PLA Royal Docks 0-6-0ST Hudswell Clarke No 1748

Manufacturer:	Hudswell, Clarke & Co Ltd
Built:	27th September 1943
Works number:	1748
Running number:	No 78 (PLA), 75089 (War Department)
At the Docks:	1944–1960

Yet another Hudswell Clarke engine swelling the ranks of those already at the Royal Docks, this one was of the War Department's "Austerity" design of 0-6-0 saddle tanks. Having begun life as WD No 75089 it was based at Kineton ammunition depot in Warwickshire until taken on loan by the PLA in May 1944 and purchased outright by them in May 1946. Running as PLA No 78 it remained at Custom House until disposed of for £532 to scrap merchants Cox & Danks Ltd at Bromley by Bow on 30th April 1960 where it was cut up in the following month.

War and Peace at the Royals

Former War Department HC No 1719 as PLA No 76 with "Austerity" companion at Custom House on 21st May 1955. (H C Casserley)

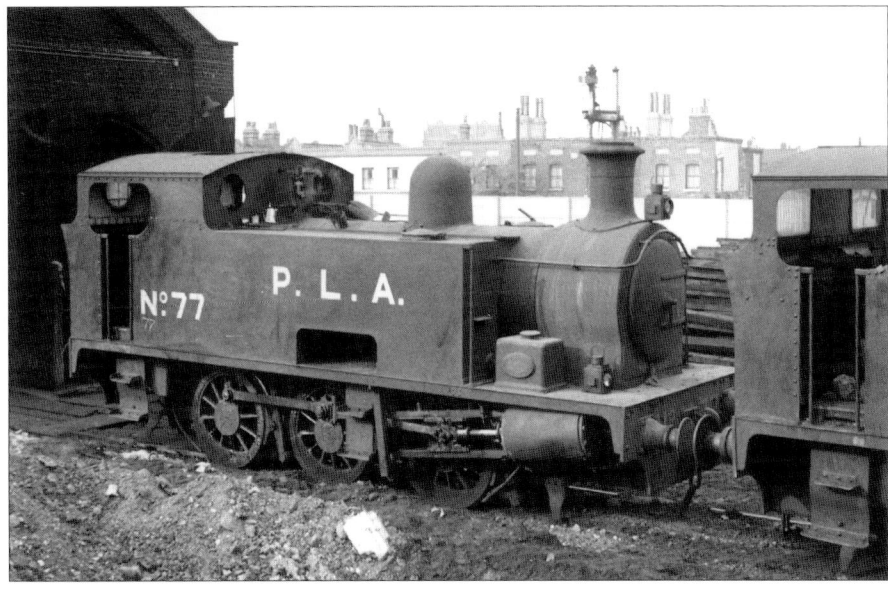

One of several War Department locos originally drafted in for assistance to the PLA during World War Two was Hudswell Clarke No 1720 seen here at Custom House on 15th September 1957. (R C Riley/Transport Treasury)

Hudswell Clarke No 1748 was another of the ex-War Department loaned engines that were later purchased by the PLA, here seen at Custom House as No 78. (Frank Jones Collection/Industrial Locomotive Society)

51

PLA Royal Docks 0-6-0ST Hunslet No 2414

Name:	(*Spitfire*)
Manufacturer:	Hunslet Engine Co Ltd
Built:	27th January 1942
Works number:	2414
Running number:	No 79 (PLA), 70066 (War Department), S112 (NCB)
Driving wheels:	4ft 0.5in
Coal capacity	2ton 0cwt
Weight:	49ton 7cwt
At the Docks:	1943–1960

Although similar to the War Department's "Austerity" class of 0-6-0 saddle tanks, this one was of a slightly different design. It was stored at Long Marston Army Depot in Warwickshire until sent on loan to the PLA at the Royal Docks in August 1943 and purchased by them in May 1946. Running as their No 79 it survived the cull of Custom House steam locos in 1960 when sold to the National Coal Board's Ackton Hall Colliery in West Yorkshire in October that year where it was renumbered S112. It was rebuilt by Hunslet in 1963 and, after working there until the summer of 1972, it was taken into preservation on the Embsay & Bolton Steam Railway in 1976 and named *Spitfire*. Following many years of static display it is currently being restored to working order and will be renamed *Revenge* when back in action.

PLA Royal Docks 0-6-0ST Hunslet No 2876

Name:	(*Jess*)
Manufacturer:	Hunslet Engine Co Ltd
Built:	14th October 1943
Works number:	2876
Running number:	No 80, (75027 War Department)
At the Docks:	1944–1960

This was another of the "Austerity" engines to find its way to Custom House. It entered War Department service as No 75027 and initially worked at Ashington Colliery, Northumberland, but in the following year was loaned to the PLA from May 1944. After the end of WWII it became another of several ex-WD loans and was purchased outright in May 1946. During that period it had been sent to Harland & Wolff at Tilbury for repairs on 20th June 1945. By 1st July 1957 it was back at the makers for a major overhaul and, after its return, worked until October 1960 when sold to the National Coal Board's Prince of Wales Colliery in North Yorkshire. After a further rebuild in 1961 a move to Waterloo Main Colliery at Leeds came on 6th September 1962 where, within six months, it had acquired the name *Jess*. Its final move, this time to Newmarket Colliery, came in November 1968, ending its days there when scrapped on site by W H Arnott Young Ltd in November 1973.

War and Peace at the Royals

Several ex-War Department saddle tanks were sent to London Docks during the latter part of the Second World War. One such loco was Hunslet No 2414 seen here at Custom House on 15th February 1958. (J G Brown/Philip J Kelley Collection)

Hunslet No 2876 was another ex-War Department loco drafted to the Royal Docks after a loan spell. Here it is pictured idle as PLA No 80 at Custom House. (Frank Jones Collection/Industrial Locomotive Society)

PLA Royal Docks 0-6-0ST Hunslet No 2881

Manufacturer:	Hunslet Engine Co Ltd
Built:	5th November 1943
Works number:	2881
Running number:	No 81 (PLA), 75032 (War Department)
At the Docks:	1944–1959

As War Department "Austerity" No 75032 this Hunslet loco was new in 1943 but was soon on loan to the PLA at the Royal Docks from May 1944. Having been purchased by them in May 1946 it remained there until withdrawn in 1958 and was scrapped on site by George Cohen Sons & Co Ltd in October 1959.

PLA Royal Docks 0-6-0ST RSH No 7103

Manufacturer:	Robert Stephenson & Hawthorns Ltd
Built:	23rd September 1943
Works number:	7103
Running number:	No 82 (75067 War Department)
At the Docks:	1944–1960

Five examples of the War Department's "Austerity" design built by Robert Stephenson & Hawthorns came to the Royal Docks on loan in 1944. No 7103 had been built by them in 1943 and sent to the PLA in February the following year. As WD No 75067 it was purchased by the docks in May 1946 and renumbered as PLA No 82. Having been rebuilt by the Hunslet Engine Company in 1956 its works plate carried the erroneous number 7113 as it worked on until November 1960 when sold to the National Coal Board's Hafod Colliery in Denbighshire. Its service at Hafod ended when scrapped there in June 1967 by Karalius Brothers of Widnes in Lancashire.

PLA Royal Docks 0-6-0ST RSH No 7104

Manufacturer:	Robert Stephenson & Hawthorns Ltd
Built:	30th September 1943
Works number:	7104
Running number:	No 83 (PLA), 75068 (War Department), 44 (NCB)
At the Docks:	1944–1960

The second RS&H loco to be loaned to the Royal Docks by the War Department was No 7104 running as WD No 75068. New in 1943 it came to Custom House in May 1944 and was purchased by the PLA in May 1946. After its service there ended in October 1960, like several others of its type, it was sold to the National Coal Board and sent to their Colliery at Ashington, Northumberland where it was renumbered 44 and ran until scrapped in August 1972.

War and Peace at the Royals

Hunslet No 2881 was one of several "Austerity" type locos sent to the Royal Docks to assist with the war effort. After being purchased by the PLA it became their No 81 and was photographed at Custom House on 4th April 1959 after being withdrawn from service. (L S Freeman/Transport Treasury)

Ex-War Department RSH No 7103 takes a breather at Custom House in its PLA days as No 82. (Frank Jones Collection/Industrial Locomotive Society)

An animated scene at Custom House shed on 21st September 1957 as RSH No 7104 (PLA No 83) gets up steam and HC No 1254 (PLA No 60) stands in line. (R C Riley/Transport Treasury)

PLA Royal Docks 0-6-0ST RSH No 7105

Manufacturer: Robert Stephenson & Hawthorns Ltd
Built: 6th October 1943
Works number: 7105
Running number: No 84 (PLA), 75069 (War Department)
At the Docks: 1944–1959

Another of the War Department "Austerity" locos built by RS&H to be loaned to the Royal Docks. This one was No 7105 which began life as WD No 75069 in 1943 and worked at Trowell Moor Old Colliery in Nottinghamshire but was soon at the docks, arriving there in January 1944. As with several others of this type, it was purchased by the PLA in May 1946, running as their No 84 until withdrawn from service in 1958 and scrapped on site by George Cohen Sons & Co Ltd in October the following year.

PLA Royal Docks 0-6-0ST RSH No 7107

Manufacturer: Robert Stephenson & Hawthorns Ltd
Built: 20th October 1943
Works number: 7107
Running number: No 85 (PLA), 75071 (War Department)
At the Docks: 1944–1959

RS&H No 7107, built in 1943, was the fourth loco from this maker to be taken on loan by the PLA from the War Department. As WD No 75071 it arrived at the Royal Docks in May 1944 and, after purchase by the Dock Authority in May 1946, became their No 85. As with two other "Austerity" types (numbers 81 and 84) it was withdrawn from service in 1958 and broken up on site by George Cohen Sons & Co Ltd in October 1959.

PLA Royal Docks 0-6-0ST RSH No 7113

Manufacturer: Robert Stephenson & Hawthorns Ltd
Built: 9th December 1943
Works number: 7113
Running number: No 86 (PLA), 75077 (War Department)
At the Docks: 1944–1960

The last of five RS&H "Austerity" locos to be loaned by the War Department to the PLA for use at the Royal Docks. As WD No 75077 when new, its military career was short lived when it was sent to Custom House in May 1944. Like several others of this type it was purchased outright by the PLA in May 1946. At the end of its time in the docks, it was sold to National Coal Board in October 1960 and accompanied three others of its kind to Ashington Colliery in Northumberland where it was eventually scrapped in March 1973.

War and Peace at the Royals

RSH No 7105 photographed in a quiet moment at Custom House on 21st September 1957 with driver George Musgrave at the cab door. (R C Riley/Transport Treasury)

RSH No 7107 with a PLA breakdown van at Custom House. (Author's collection)

RSH No 7113 with a train at Custom House on 14th March 1958. (Alec Swain/Transport Treasury)

London's Dock Railways: The Royal Docks, North Woolwich and Silvertown

The PLA created a central Railway Department under which all dock movements were administered and, around 1912, the post of Railway Superintendent was created to oversee the whole of the docks railway system and be responsible to the Chief Docks Manager, who, in turn, reported to the General Manager. His office was at Custom House, to the north of the Royal Victoria Dock and, under his supervision, there were three Senior Traffic Officers, one for each of the operational centres at Millwall (later, India and Millwall), Royals, and Tilbury, each having a locomotive shed. Railway Traffic Officers dealt with the local quay and shed operations while activities at the running sheds came under the jurisdiction of the Chief Engineers Department, where, in the 1930s, were housed a total of 27 locos but within two decades the number had risen to 46 with 22 at the Royal Docks, 14 at Tilbury and 10 at Millwall. The Royal Docks railway movements were controlled from a cabin on a bridge over the exchange sidings. Repairs to locomotives was outsourced to Harland & Wolff while new track work and track maintenance was undertaken by contractors John Mowlem & Co.

From the days of the dock companies, the railway companies had been granted rights of access to the docks systems for the running of passenger trains to various berths and this dispensation was continued under the PLA, especially with boat trains to the quaysides at the Royal Group which served Cunard White Star, Orient, Atlantic Transport and P&O. In the 1950s these could number up to four specials per ship, each with up to 300 passengers. P&O boat trains often consisted of nine coaches.

Special Boat Trains ran mostly from Liverpool Street, Fenchurch Street and St Pancras and, after entering the docks en-route to the quaysides, the Ministry of Transport's regulations required points to be locked and flagmen placed on the route. Ticketing varied from dock to dock. At the Royals, the PLA issued its own tickets often from temporary booths but passengers could also purchase them on board ship.

At the Royal Victoria Docks rail movements were monitored from a control centre based in a cabin on a bridge over the exchange sidings. (PLA)

Above: The Custom House running shed at Victoria Docks with assembled inmates on 4th April 1959. (Jack Faithfull, RCTS)

Left: LMS No 4210 in the early days of BR on the south side of the King George V Dock with a boat train from St Pancras. (PLA/Colin Withey Collection)

London's Dock Railways: The Royal Docks, North Woolwich and Silvertown

By the 1950s the PLA wagon count had changed a little, then made up of 310 open trucks, 38 box vans, 120 flat wagons 77 insulated vans, 3 brake vans (for use at the Connaught tunnel), one breakdown van, a weed killer wagon and two special wagons for transporting glass. All of these were strictly limited to internal use between quays and sheds etc and were never allowed on to the main lines due to their generally lower standards of design and maintenance. The overall wagon and van livery was dark red with the exception of the insulated vans, which were pale chrome or yellow, and the flat wagons (used mainly for timber transportation in the India and Millwall Docks) that were grey.

Also, during the 1950s, the Royal Docks suffered a shortage of locos, mainly due to the run down state and poor maintenance of its regular stock, so a few "outsiders" were brought in to lend assistance between 1952 and 1956. Among these were War Department numbers 106 (HE 2889), 108 (HE 2891), 136 (HE 3172) and 142 (WB 2739), together with Peckett No 2025 and several BR locos sent over from nearby Stratford shed. Those noted were J67 class numbers 68549 and 68563, J69s 68574, 68578, 68621 and 68631 and J68s 68644 and 68654.

Other PLA engines were transferred from Tilbury Docks as HE numbers 2878 (87) and 3166 (88), HC numbers 1873 (90) and 1874 (91), HL No 3529 (69) and HC No 1103 (70) all arrived between 1954 and 1959. By then the Royals had moved into dieselisation with 12 new locos arriving at Custom House from the Yorkshire Engine Company in 1959 along with four others brought over from Tilbury in that year, and lastly, a final YE coming from the Essex port in 1968.

PLA "Austerity" No 78 (HC No 1748) hauls a train of refrigerated meat vans at Z Shed in the Royal Victoria Docks in 1949. (PLA/Colin Withey Collection)

War and Peace at the Royals

Another glimpse of the Royal Docks in 1949 as PLA No 85 (RSH No 7107) traverses the quayside. (PLA/Colin Withey Collection)

One of the BR locos supplied periodically from Stratford shed to assist with shortages at the Royal Docks. PLA Driver George Musgrave stands beside J68 class No 68654 at Custom House. (George Musgrave/Colin Withey Collection)

PLA Royal Docks Loan 0-6-0ST Hunslet No 2891

Name:	*(Jullundur)*
Manufacturer:	Hunslet Engine Co Ltd
Built:	1943
Works number:	2891
Running number:	No 34 (LMR), 75042 and 108 (both War Department)
At the Docks:	1952–1954

New to the War Department in 1943, Hunslet No 2891 was originally allocated the name *Lord Gort* but this had changed to *Jullundur* by the time it arrived at the Longmoor Military Railway in February 1946. Having been rebuilt by the makers in 1952 it became one of several "Austerity" locos loaned to the Port of London Authority. It was at the Royal Docks from 17th December 1952 until 2nd September 1954 where it shared duties with HE 2889 for several months before returning to Longmoor. After another overhaul by Hunslet between April and September 1956 it returned to Longmoor for its final years before being sold for scrap to Woodham Brothers at Barry Docks in July 1963 for a final sad reunion with HE 2889 before being broken up by March 1965.

PLA Royal Docks Loan 0-6-0ST Hunslet No 2889

Name:	*(Spyck)*
Manufacturer:	Hunslet Engine Co Ltd
Built:	1943
Works number:	2889
Running number:	No 32 (LMR), 75040 and 106 (both War Department)
At the Docks:	1954

One of many "Austerity" wartime locomotives, Hunslet No 2889 carried the name *Spyck* during its military service until 1952. Having been delivered new to the War Department in 1943 it was observed at the Marchwood Military Railway in 1948 and was at Longmoor the following year. From there it was loaned to the Port of London Authority between 22nd February and 22nd July in 1954 where it teamed up with HE 2891 for a few months, before returning to the military and being sighted at Marchwood in May 1955. In October that year it had been sent to the makers for a rebuild, returning to Marchwood in May 1956 before a final transfer to Longmoor in June 1960. After being sold for scrap to Woodham Brothers at Barry Docks in July 1963 it was eventually dismantled in March 1965 along with sister HE No 2891.

PLA Royal Docks 0-6-0ST Hunslet No 3172

Manufacturer:	Hunslet Engine Co Ltd
Built:	1944
Works number:	3172
Running number:	75122 and 136 (both War Department)
At the Docks:	1955–1956

Hunslet No 3172 was one of several locos taken on loan by the PLA during a shortage of motive power at the Royal Docks in the mid 1950s. New from the makers on 15th June 1944 it entered War Department service as No 75122 at Sudbury Central Vehicle Depot, Staffordshire before being hired to the PLA in August 1955. By October the next year it was at the Army's Bicester workshops, remaining there until a move to Bramley Ammunition Depot in Hampshire came in July 1957. After leaving Bramley in March 1961 it was placed in store from September 1961 until sold to the National Coal Board's Ashington Colliery, Northumberland, in March 1962. Its career in the coal industry took it to collieries at Shilbottle, Backworth, and finally Burradon in January 1976 where it was scrapped on site by C H Newton Jnr & Co Ltd in April that year.

War and Peace at the Royals

One of several War Department locos loaned to the PLA was Hunslet No 2891, seen here in its Longmoor Military Railway livery at Custom House on 12th June 1954. (L S Freeman/Transport Treasury)

Longmoor Military Railway No 106 (HE No 2889) was on loan to the PLA in 1954 and is pictured at Custom House on 12th June that year. (L S Freeman/Transport Treasury)

PLA Royal Docks 0-6-0ST Bagnall No 2739

Name:	*(The Craftsman)*
Manufacturer:	W G Bagnall, Stafford.
Built:	1944
Works number:	2739
Running number:	75151 and 142 (both War Department)
At the Docks:	1956

A Bagnall example of the War Department "Austerity" design, No 2739 was supplied on 29th May 1944 for wartime service. Between September 1953 and October 1955 it was at the Bicester Military Railway in Oxfordshire and carried the name *The Craftsman* from June 1954 until it was loaned to the PLA in February 1956. It afterwards went into storage at the Royal Engineers' Bicester Workshops until June 1959, when, surplus to requirements, it was sold for scrap to Thomas W Ward at Grays in Essex and broken up some time after September 1960.

A rare snapshot of Bagnall No 2739 (WD No 142) on hire to the Royal Docks with PLA driver George Musgrave in the foreground. (George Musgrave/Colin Withey Collection)

PLA Royal Docks 0-4-0ST Peckett No 2025

Name:	*(Charles)*
Manufacturer:	Peckett & Sons Ltd
Built:	17th August 1942
Works number:	2025
Cylinders:	14in x 22in
Driving Wheels:	3ft 2.5in
Boiler Pressure:	160psi
Wheelbase:	5ft 6in
Weight:	24ton 0cwt
At the Docks:	1953–1954

This loco was new to the Royal Ordnance Factory at Hirwaun, South Glamorgan. The factory closed in November 1945 and by 22nd August 1946 the site had been taken over by the Wales & Monmouthshire Industrial Estates Ltd as Hirwaun Trading Estate. On 27th March 1953 it was sold to the firm of Abelson (Engineers) Ltd at Birmingham from where it was loaned to the PLA at Custom House between December 1953 and February 1954. After returning to Abelson it was sold by them to the Llanelly Steel Co Ltd, Carmarthenshire sometime between June 1955 and April 1957 where it was named *Charles*, working on until scrapped there around 1968.

War and Peace at the Royals

One of the principal cargoes at the Royal Docks was meat and PLA No 64 (HC No 1414) is seen hauling a train of London & South Western Railway refrigerated vans at Custom House in the 1920s. (Colin Withey Collection)

Not all dock movements were by PLA locomotives. Here, Midland Region 3F No 47489 enters the exchange sidings at Victoria Docks with a train of BR stock. (PLA/Colin Withey Collection)

London's Dock Railways: The Royal Docks, North Woolwich and Silvertown

Dock freight comes in all types, in this case, heavy! PLA No 77 (HC No 1720) hauls a 70 ton transformer on a 24-wheeled wagon at the Royal Docks Exchange Sidings in 1947. (PLA/Colin Withey Collection)

Looking east to the King George V Dock in 1951 with the "Dominion Monarch" in drydock. On the left is the Royal Albert Dock. This vast area was destined to become the new London City Airport in a later existence. (PLA)

War and Peace at the Royals

The Custom House engineering works at Victoria Docks were leased to Harland & Wolff who carried out major repairs to PLA locos there from 1921. PLA No 65 (HC No 1415) lends a helping hand to one of its sisters there on 21st May 1955. A string of internal wagons stands outside. (H C Casserley)

Another scene at the Custom House workshops on 21st May 1955. A mobile Smiths steam crane, a remnant of days gone by, stands near to a discarded jib and a dismembered saddle tank from one of the PLA's "Austerity" locos. On the right is an office belonging to Harland & Wolff who carried out major repairs and maintenance of the PLA stock. (H C Casserley)

London's Dock Railways: The Royal Docks, North Woolwich and Silvertown

"Austerity" RSH No 7103 steams past Custom House running shed with a train of PLA stock on 25th September 1957. (R C Riley/Transport Treasury)

Autumn days for steam as PLA "Austerity" No 82 (RSH No 7103) heads past the running sheds and workshops at Custom House on 25th September 1957. Others in the photo appear to be locos No 73 (HC No 1598) to the rear and No 77 (HC No 1720) over at the shed (R C Riley/Transport Treasury)

War and Peace at the Royals

HC No 1254 (PLA No 60) with a train passing signal box "D" adjacent to the Custom House workshops on 25th September 1957. (R C Riley/Transport Treasury)

A visit to Custom House shed in June 1953 revealed 22 locos on site with 18 working and three more under repair, while another was out of use there. Rumours of the impending dieselisation of the docks motive power had been circulating that year and, to the dismay of some of the stalwart loco men, a diesel loco had been on trials, but it proved unsatisfactory and, surprisingly, two more steam locos, HC numbers 1873 (90) and 1875 (91) were ordered for Tilbury in 1954 while Peckett No 2025 arrived at Custom House for a short loan. However, the inevitable was merely postponed until 1956 when the new breed arrived at Tilbury, after which they appeared at Custom House just three years later.

On 25th September 1954 in the Royal Docks there were 19 locos hard at work with four more, HL 3529 (67), HE 2414 (79), RSH 7104 (83) and HC 1155 (52) all under repair. HE No 2878 (87) had arrived from Tilbury on 17th July that year for overhaul and a new boiler, with HE 3166 (87) following it there in November. Outside the workshops were various parts of numbers 67 and either 79 or 83. Such was the call on locos at that time, the working engines were described as being in dirty condition: even those that had been quite recently repainted.

As previously mentioned, five locos were also on hire during the mid 1950s. Peckett No 2025 from the Birmingham firm of Abelson, along with "Austerities" WD numbers 106 (HE 2889), 108 (HE 2891), 136 (HE 3172) and 142 (WB 2739) from the military. As a result of diesels being introduced at Tilbury, the two "almost new" HC locos numbers 1873 (90) and 1874 (91) were transferred from there to Custom House in January and July 1957 respectively. For the same reason, HL No 3529 (69) took the same route in 1958 but its reprieve lasted only until it was scrapped just two years later.

One of the later recorded shed visits to Custom House was made on 12th October 1957 when a total of 28 locomotives were assembled, including five that had come from Tilbury following the change to diesels there. Working locos (or at least those capable of work) were numbers 51, 62, 63, 65, 66, 67, 68, 72, 76, 77, 79, 84, 86 and 87, while at the workshops was No 73 under heavy repair along with the dismembered No 78 having attention to its boiler. Outside was the remains of No 52 having been scrapped earlier that year and a derelict No

Hudswell Clarke No 1748 as PLA No 78 passes the Dock Manager's Office at Custom House in 1948. (PLA/Colin Withey Collection)

71. No 85 was stored on a siding awaiting a trip to Hunslet for rebuilding. With the impending arrival of diesel locos at Custom House some hope was given for the reprieve of steam locos that were fitted for steam heating the banana traffic at the Royal and Millwall Docks but that would only last until 1963.

The first diesels at Custom House came from the Yorkshire Engine Company as numbers 2690, 2691, 2739, 2740, 2758, 2759, 2761, 2762, 2763, 2769 and 2770 were delivered new from mid 1959 through to early 1960 when, in April that year, HC No 1874 (91) was sent to end its days at Millwall. The diesel fleet was augmented by four others, numbers 2619, 2620, 2633 and 2640, that had transferred from Tilbury in October 1959 and a final addition was No 2630, also arriving from Tilbury in 1968.

The previous numbering of steam locos had ended at No 91 and, to distinguish the new diesel stock, the PLA began their series from No 200, which ran to No 240 across the various docks. All those at the Royal Docks were six-coupled and the first four were of the powerful 440hp Janus type, their main dimensions being:

Engine: 400hp 2xRR C6SFL
Driving Wheels: 3ft 8in
Wheelbase: 11ft 0in
Weight: 49ton 0cwt

The other 0-6-0 types were:
Engine: 300hp RR C8SFL
Driving Wheels: 3ft 3in
Wheelbase: 9ft 0in
Weight: 30ton 0cwt

In the wake of their arrival, most of the remaining steamers were condemned and sold, while just a few were retained for the heating of banana of trains. In terms of steam locomotives, many of the old guard were relatively young when disposed of in the 1960s, a good number going to the scrap firm if Mayer, Newman & Co. Across all docks, around 20 were less than two decades old and three had seen less than 10 years service. No less than 41 locos were disposed of after the diesels first appeared, the final four hanging on until 1963.

Royal Docks steam locomotives purchased by PLA

Maker	Works No	Type	PLA No	Date Arrived	Date Departed	Notes
AB	1236	0-6-0T	38	1911	1951	Scrapped
AB	1237	0-6-0T	39	1911	1951	Scrapped
AB	1294	0-6-0T	41	1912	1946	Scrapped
AB	1300	0-6-0T	42	1912	1948	Sold
AB	1301	0-6-0T	43	1912	1948	Sold
AB	1302	0-6-0T	44	1913	1953	Sold for Scrap
HC	1153	0-6-0T	50	1915	1947	Scrapped
HC	1154	0-6-0T	51	1915	1960	Scrapped
HC	1155	0-6-0T	52	1915	1956	Scrapped
HC	1244	0-6-0T	58	1917	1960	Scrapped
HC	1245	0-6-0T	59	1917	1960	Scrapped
HC	1254	0-6-0T	60	1917	1960	Scrapped
HC	1255	0-6-0T	61	1917	1947	Sold
HC	1323	0-6-0T	62	1918	1960	Scrapped
HC	1324	0-6-0T	63	1918	1959	Scrapped
HC	1414	0-6-0T	64	1920	1953	Scrapped
HC	1415	0-6-0T	65	1920	1960	Sold for Scrap
HC	1453	0-6-0T	66	1921	1960	Sold for Scrap
HC	1454	0-6-0T	67/73	1921	1963	Sold for Scrap
HC	1455	0-6-0T	68	1921	1960	Sold for Scrap
HC	1596	0-6-0T	71	1927	1959	Scrapped
HC	1597	0-6-0T	72	1927	1961	Scrapped
HC	1598	0-6-0T	73	1927	1960	Scrapped
HC	1719	0-6-0T	76	1943	1961	Scrapped
HC	1720	0-6-0T	77	1943	1960	Scrapped
HC	1748	0-6-0ST	78	1944	1960	Sold for Scrap
HE	2414	0-6-0ST	79	1943	1960	Sold
HE	2876	0-6-0ST	80	1944	1960	Sold
HE	2881	0-6-0ST	81	1944	1959	Scrapped
RSHN	7103	0-6-0ST	82	1944	1960	Sold
RSHN	7104	0-6-0ST	83	1944	1960	Sold
RSHN	7105	0-6-0ST	84	1944	1959	Scrapped
RSHN	7107	0-6-0ST	85	1944	1959	Scrapped
RSHN	7113	0-6-0ST	86	1944	1960	Sold

Sunset on the PLA steam era as a line of 16 condemned locos await their fate at Custom House on 30th April 1960. (R C Riley/Transport Treasury)

Above: *The new breed at the PLA sees YE No 2690 (PLA No 206) with driver George Musgrave and head shunter R Grant aboard. (George Musgrave/Colin Withey Collection)*

Opposite: *The halcyon days of ships and railways are drawing to a close as one of the YE "Janus" locos hauls a train through the Royal Docks c1965. (PLA)*

War and Peace at the Royals

London's Dock Railways: The Royal Docks, North Woolwich and Silvertown

Left: A condemned Hudswell Clarke No 1719, coupled with comparative newcomer PLA No 237 (YE No 2762), at the Royal Docks on 21st January 1961. (© 2010 - 53A Models of Hull Collection/R. Munday)

Below: New facilities for the diesel era at Custom House lasted only a decade before rail traffic was abandoned in 1970. Two of the YE locos are pictured there on 31st August 1964. (Roger Hateley)

War and Peace at the Royals

Above: Three of the YE Diesels, numbers 2760, 2619 and 2759 (PLA numbers 235, 200 and 234), were not exactly overworked in this scene at the Royal Docks on 31st August 1964. (Roger Hateley)

Left: Assorted wagons at the exchange sidings north of the Victoria Docks during the final era of diesel loco working. (PLA)

London's Dock Railways: The Royal Docks, North Woolwich and Silvertown

Modern workshops were provided at Custom House to maintain the newcomers, but their reign was short lived. Changes in shipping methods to containerisation, and the growing switch of freight to road transport saw rail movements dwindle. The great modernisation of the docks railways was to no avail. The cessation of the PLA railways was announced on 1st May 1970 after which the majority of movements entailed the removal of stock and the lifting of redundant miles of track. After various periods in storage all of the PLA diesel locos were eventually sold on to other industrial concerns.

The Royal Docks remained open for another decade, which saw shipping decline with closure coming in 1981. For a couple more years the desolate quays accommodated vessels on lay up until the entire estate was sold and redeveloped under the guidance of the London Docks Development Corporation. By 1987 much of the site had become the London City Airport with the surrounding areas revamped as housing and parkland.

Above: PLA rail mounted diesel crane No DL12 assists in unloading at the Royal Docks around 1960. (PLA/Colin Withey Collection)

Right: YE No 2633 as PLA No 203 at work in the Victoria Docks at E and F sheds. (PLA/Colin Withey Collection)

The view eastwards across the Royal Docks in 1965 with the Royal Victoria Docks in the foreground and the Royal Albert and King George V Docks in the distance. (PLA)

PLA Royal Docks 0-6-0DE Yorkshire "Janus" No 2690

Manufacturer:	Yorkshire Engine Company
Built:	7th May 1959
Works number:	2690
Running number:	206 (PLA), 95 (Tata Steel)
At the Docks:	1959–1970

New the Royal Docks in 1959 this loco saw its entire dock service there until closure saw it sold to the Richard Thomas & Baldwin's Redbourn steelworks at Scunthorpe, Lincolnshire on 17th June 1970. From November 1972 it was with Appleby Frodingham at Scunthorpe, and after the site being taken over by several successive steel companies it is still employed there by Tata Steel as their No 95.

PLA Royal Docks 0-6-0DE Yorkshire "Janus" No 2691

Manufacturer:	Yorkshire Engine Company
Built:	14th May 1959
Works number:	2691
Running number:	207 (PLA)
At the Docks:	1959–1970

Another of the batch of powerful "Janus" type locos delivered to Custom House in 1959. On closure of the docks railway this one was sold to the Workington Iron & Steel Company's Moss Bay Works at Cumberland in June 1970 where it lasted until dismantled around 1983.

PLA Royal Docks 0-6-0DE Yorkshire "Janus" No 2739

Manufacturer:	Yorkshire Engine Company
Built:	27th May 1959
Works number:	2739
Running number:	208 (PLA)
At the Docks:	1959–1971

One of the initial batch of "Janus" locos supplied to the PLA's Royal Docks in 1959, seeing its service there ended when sold to the British Steel Corporation's Tinsley Park Works at Sheffield in May 1971. It then moved to the company's nearby Stocksbridge Works where it was finally scrapped sometime in 2000.

PLA Royal Docks 0-6-0DE Yorkshire "Janus" No 2740

Manufacturer:	Yorkshire Engine Company
Built:	4th June 1959
Works number:	2740
Running number:	209 (PLA), 33 (British Steel)
At the Docks:	1959–1971

As with others of its class this loco was sent to work in the Royal Docks in 1959 and its short career there ended when sold to Shell Mex & BP Ltd at Killingholme, Lincolnshire around March 1971. On 15th July 1977 it went to the works of Thomas Hill at Kilnhurst from where it was sold to British Steel's Stocksbridge works, Sheffield, on 23rd February 1978 where it was renumbered 33 and still remains in service.

War and Peace at the Royals

YE No 2691 stands amongst its sisters at Custom House on 21st January 1961. (© 2010 - 53A Models of Hull Collection/R Munday)

Custom House on 21st January 1961 where YE No 2740 as PLA no 209 awaits a turn of duty. (© 2010 - 53A Models of Hull Collection/R Munday)

PLA Royal Docks 0-6-0DE Yorkshire No 2758

Name:	*(Glastonbury)*
Manufacturer:	Yorkshire Engine Company
Built:	25th November 1959
Works number:	2758
Running number:	233 (PLA), 381 (GKN)
At the Docks:	1959–1971

One of the later diesel arrivals at Custom House, this one served the docks until the railway closed, being subsequently sold off with several others to GKN's Tremorfa Steelworks at South Glamorgan in 1971. After being renumbered 381 and named *Glastonbury* it was eventually scrapped on site there by the firm of Slag Reduction Ltd together with sister No 2762 in June 1981.

PLA Royal Docks 0-6-0DE Yorkshire No 2759

Manufacturer:	Yorkshire Engine Company
Built:	26th October 1959
Works number:	2759
Running number:	234 (PLA)
At the Docks:	1959–1972

One of many new YE locos that had a relatively short lived career at the Royal Docks. After arriving in 1959 it lasted only until sold to the Sheerness Iron & Steel Company Ltd at Sheerness in Kent in May 1972, remaining there until scrapped about 1983.

PLA Royal Docks 0-6-0DE Yorkshire No 2760

Name:	*(Bamborough)*
Manufacturer:	Yorkshire Engine Company
Built:	25th November 1959
Works number:	2760
Running number:	235 (PLA), 372 (GKN)
At the Docks:	1959–1971

Arriving new to Custom House in 1959 its relatively short working life there ended in March 1971 when it was sold, along with many others, to the GKN's Tremorfa Steelworks in South Glamorgan. There it was renumbered 372 and named *Bamborough* before retirement to the Gloucester Warwickshire Railway Society at Toddington, moving there sometime between 22nd October and 5th November 1999.

PLA Royal Docks 0-6-0DE Yorkshire No 2761

Name:	*(Lemanis)*
Manufacturer:	Yorkshire Engine Company
Built:	14th December 1959
Works number:	2761
Running number:	236 (PLA), 396 (GKN)
At the Docks:	1959–1973

A late arrival at Custom House in 1959 where it joined others of its type for an all too brief career at the Royal Docks. As with the others it was disposed of after the dock railway closed in 1970 and sold with several others to GKN's Tremorfa steelworks at South Glamorgan in 1973. There it was given the number 396 and carried the name *Lemanis* before being sold to the Rover Group Ltd at Swindon, Wiltshire, between 20th October 1993 and 25th February 1994. Sometime after 29th April 1994 it moved to Cooper Metals at Swindon and, on 20th February 1999, it went to the Yorkshire Engine Company at Long Marston, Warwickshire, for repairs, returning on 30th April the following year. By 29th July 2000 it was back with YE before being sold to the firm of John Payne at Long Marston in November 2001 where its time was short before being scrapped on site by Stratford Car Breakers in May 2002.

PLA Royal Docks 0-6-0DE Yorkshire No 2762

Name:	*(Llongporth)*
Manufacturer:	Yorkshire Engine Company
Built:	21st December 1959
Works number:	2762
Running number:	237 (PLA), 373 (GKN)
At the Docks:	1959–1971

Yet another of the YE locos that arrived new at the Royal Docks in 1959 but enjoyed only a short lived career there until sold after the dock railway closed in 1970. In April 1971 it became one of the many such PLA diesels purchased by the GKN's Tremorfa steelworks in South Glamorgan. There is was numbered 373 and named *Llongporth* until being scrapped on site with sister No 2758 by the firm of Slag Reduction Ltd in June 1981.

One of the standard 0-6-0DE types to work at Custom House was YE No 2761 seen here as PLA No 236 on 21st January 1961. (© 2010 - 53A Models of Hull Collection/R Munday)

PLA Royal Docks 0-6-0DE Yorkshire No 2763

Name:	*(Kin-Kenadon)*
Manufacturer:	Yorkshire Engine Company
Built:	21st December 1959
Works number:	2763
Running number:	238 (PLA), 371 (GKN)
At the Docks:	1959–1971

One of the batch of diesel locos supplied to the PLA for use at the Royal Docks that arrived new in 1959. After working there for six years as PLA No 238 it was transferred to Millwall, being the last arrival there, where it continued in service until the rail system closed in 1970. As with all the other PLA diesels, it was sold on to another industrial concern, in this case to the GKN works at Tremorfa in South Glamorgan in February 1971 where it carried the number 371 and was named *Kin-Kenadon* until sold to dealers Wilmott Brothers, Ilkeston Plant Depot, Derbyshire on 25th July 1993 where it was scrapped the following January.

PLA Royal Docks 0-6-0DE Yorkshire No 2769

Name:	*(Calleva)*
Manufacturer:	Yorkshire Engine Company
Built:	6th January 1960
Works number:	2769
Running number:	239 (PLA), 398 (GKN)
At the Docks:	1960–1973

Although officially built in 1959 this loco was one of the last to arrive at the Royal Docks early in 1960. It was also one of the last to leave when sold to GKN's Tremorfa steelworks in South Glamorgan in 1973. During its time there it took the name *Calleva* and ran as No 398 until sold to Wilmott Bros (Plant Services) Ilkston Depot in Derbyshire sometime between 9th April and 4th July 1996. It was then with the Llangollen Railway from August 2000 where it was stored at West Hallam until sent for scrap to EMR at Kingsbury, Tamworth, on 29th November 2010.

PLA Royal Docks 0-6-0DE Yorkshire No 2770

Name:	*(Cunetio)*
Manufacturer:	Yorkshire Engine Company
Built:	11th January 1960
Works number:	2770
Running number:	240 (PLA), 394 (GKN)
At the Docks:	1960–1972

A second loco built in 1959 but delivered new to Custom House in early 1960. It became yet another of the many PLA locos sold to the GKN Tremorfa Steelworks at South Glamorgan, leaving for its new owners in May 1972. As with all the others it was given a name, in this case *Cunetio,* and renumbered as 394. It days there ended when scrapped on site by the local Cardiff firm of Allied Bird Fragmentation Ltd in December 1994.

War and Peace at the Royals

Yorkshire Engine Co No 2763 as PLA No 238 working at the Royal Docks in 1959. (Brian Webb Collection / Industrial Railway Society)

Royal Docks diesel locomotives purchased by PLA

Maker	Works No	Type	PLA No	Date Arrived	Date Departed	Notes
YE	2690	0-6-0DE	206	1959	1970	Sold
YE	2691	0-6-0DE	207	1959	1970	Sold
YE	2739	0-6-0DE	208	1959	1971	Sold
YE	2740	0-6-0DE	209	1959	1971	Sold
YE	2758	0-6-0DE	233	1959	1971	Sold
YE	2759	0-6-0DE	234	1959	1972	Sold
YE	2760	0-6-0DE	235	1959	1971	Sold
YE	2761	0-6-0DE	236	1959	1973	Sold
YE	2762	0-6-0DE	237	1959	1971	Sold
YE	2763	0-6-0DE	238	1959	1971	Sold
YE	2769	0-6-0DE	239	1960	1973	Sold
YE	2770	0-6-0DE	240	1960	1972	Sold

London's Dock Railways: The Royal Docks, North Woolwich and Silvertown

The long and colourful era of London's Dock Railways had finally passed into history and the following list is an impressive summary of all the locomotives purchased by the various dock companies and those of the Port of London Authority that succeeded them:

All Company Purchases in order of appearance

Maker	Works No	Name	Type	Dock Company	Dock Allocated	Running Number	Date Arrived	PLA Number	Date Departed
MW	423	*Primus*	0-4-0ST	MD	Millwall	-	1873	16	1919
MW	?		0-4-0ST	MD	Millwall	?1	?	-	?
Shanks	?	*Victoria*	0-4-0ST	L&StKD	Royal	9	1878	-	1896
Shanks	?	*Albert*	0-4-0ST	L&StKD	Royal	10	1878	-	1902
Shanks	?		0-4-0ST	MD	Millwall	2	1879	-	1912
JF	3807	*Swift*	0-6-0ST	E&WID	West Ind	-	1880	26	1914
MW	749		2-4-0T	MD	MER	3	1880	28	1922
MW	750		2-4-0T	MD	MER	4	1880	29	1922
MW	776		2-4-0T	MD	MER	6	1880	31	1922
MW	727		0-4-0ST	MD	Millwall	5	1880	30	1919
MW	752		0-4-0ST	MD	Millwall	7	1880	32	1919
Bton	?	*Chelsea*	0-6-0ST	L&StKD	Royal	-	1880	-	?1880
D	1438		0-6-0ST	L&StKD	Royal	1	1881	1	1917
D	1439		0-6-0ST	L&StKD	Royal	2	1881	2	1920
D	1440		0-6-0ST	L&StKD	Royal	3	1881	3	1917
D	1441		0-6-0ST	L&StKD	Royal	4	1881	4	1920
Crewe	?		2-4-0T	L&StKD	RADPS	5	1881	-	1896
Crewe	?		2-4-0T	L&StKD	RADPS	6	1881	-	1896
Crewe	?		2-4-0T	L&StKD	RADPS	7	1881	-	1896
Longridge	?	*Long Wind*	0-6-0ST	L&StKD	Royal	8	1881	-	1898
FW	149		0-6-0ST	L&StKD	Royal	11	1882	11	1913
MW	876		0-4-0ST	MD	Millwall	8	1883	33	1914
FW	288		0-6-0ST	L&StKD	Royal	12	1883	12	1913
FW	263		0-6-0ST	L&StKD	Royal	13	1883	13	1917
YE	284		0-4-0ST	L&StKD	Royal	14	1883	14	1917
MW	893		0-4-0ST	L&StKD	Royal	16	1883	-	1900
FE	?		0-4-0ST	L&StKD	Royal	15	1884	15	1914
MW	905		0-4-0ST	L&StKD	Royal	9	1884	16	1920
RP	?		0-4-0ST	L&StKD	Royal	18	1884	18	1912
HE	343		0-4-0ST	L&StKD	Royal	10	1884	10	1910
FE	?		0-4-0tram	L&StKD	Royal	20	1884	-	1900
MW	663	*Ant*	0-6-0ST	E&WID	Tilbury	1	1886	-	1907
MW	694	*Bat*	0-6-0ST	E&WID	Tilbury	4	1886	17	1919
MW	872	*Wasp*	0-6-0ST	E&WID	Tilbury	3	1886	18	1919
MW	873	*Fly*	0-6-0ST	E&WID	Tilbury	7	1886	19	1919
HE	234	*Moth*	0-6-0ST	E&WID	Tilbury	6	1886	27	1912
HE	235	*Bee*	0-6-0ST	E&WID	Tilbury	2	1886	-	1914
MW	1008		0-4-0ST	MD	Millwall	9	1887	34	1927
MW	1106		0-4-0ST	MD	Millwall	10	1888	35	1926
RS	2844		0-6-0ST	L&IDJC	Tilbury	5	1896	5	1937
RS	2845		0-6-0ST	L&IDJC	Tilbury	6	1896	6	1926
RS	2981		0-6-0ST	L&IDJC	Tilbury	7	1900	7	1929
RS	2982	*Agenor*	0-6-0ST	L&IDJC	Tilbury	8	1900	8	1929
RS	2983		0-6-0ST	L&IDJC	Tilbury	9	1900	9	1926
P	851		0-4-0ST	MD	Millwall	11	1901	36	1927
P	897		0-4-0ST	MD	Millwall	12	1901	37	1927

War and Peace at the Royals

Maker	Works No	Name	Type	Dock Company	Dock Allocated	Running Number	Date Arrived	PLA Number	Date Departed
RS	3070		0-6-0ST	L&IDC	Royal	10	1901	10	1951
RS	3050	*Looe*	0-6-0ST	L&IDC	Royal	11	1901	11	1950
RS	3053	*Ajax*	0-6-0ST	L&IDC	Tilbury	2	1901	21	1934
RS	3094		0-6-0ST	L&IDC	Royal	12	1902	12	1931
RS	3120	*Hector*	0-6-0ST	L&IDC	Tilbury	-	1904	22	1932
RS	3170	*Jason*	0-6-0ST	L&IDC	Tilbury	-	1905	23	1937
RS	3296	*Nestor*	0-6-0ST	L&IDC	Tilbury	-	1907	24	1938
AB	1236		0-6-0T	PLA	Royal		1911	38	1951
AB	1237		0-6-0T	PLA	Royal		1911	39	1951
AB	1238		0-6-0T	PLA	Tilbury		1911	40	1952
AB	1294		0-6-0T	PLA	Royal		1912	41	1946
AB	1300		0-6-0T	PLA	Royal		1912	42	1948
AB	1301		0-6-0T	PLA	Royal		1912	43	1948
AB	1302		0-6-0T	PLA	Royal		1913	44	1953
HC	1101		0-6-0T	PLA	Tilbury		1915	45	1959
HC	1102		0-6-0T	PLA	Tilbury		1915	46	1942
HC	1103		0-6-0T	PLA	Tilbury		1915	49	1961
HC	1104		0-4-0ST	PLA	Millwall		1915	47	1962
HC	1105		0-4-0ST	PLA	Millwall		1915	48	1962
HC	1123		0-4-0ST	PLA	Millwall		1915	53	1962
HC	1153		0-6-0T	PLA	Royal		1915	50	1948
HC	1154		0-6-0T	PLA	Royal		1915	51	1960
HC	1155		0-6-0T	PLA	Royal		1915	52	1956
HC	1176		0-4-0ST	PLA	Millwall		1915	54	1962
HC	1177		0-4-0ST	PLA	Millwall		1915	55	1961
HL	3176		0-4-0ST	PLA	Millwall		1916	56	1962
HL	3177		0-4-0ST	PLA	Millwall		1916	57	1962
HC	1244		0-6-0T	PLA	Royal		1917	58	1960
HC	1245		0-6-0T	PLA	Royal		1917	59	1960
HC	1254		0-6-0T	PLA	Royal		1917	60	1960
HC	1255		0-6-0T	PLA	Royal		1917	61	1947
HC	1323		0-6-0T	PLA	Royal		1918	62	1960
HC	1324		0-6-0T	PLA	Royal		1918	63	1959
HC	1414		0-6-0T	PLA	Royal		1920	64	1953
HC	1415		0-6-0T	PLA	Royal		1920	65	1960
HC	1453		0-6-0T	PLA	Royal		1921	66	1960
HC	1454		0-6-0T	PLA	Royal		1921	67	1963
HC	1455		0-6-0T	PLA	Royal		1921	68	1960
Sdn	?		0-4-0VBT	PLA	MER		1921	Car 1	1928
Sdn	?		0-4-0VBT	PLA	MER		1921	Car 2	1928
HL	2650		0-6-0VBT	PLA	MER		1921	Car 3	1928
HL	3529		0-6-0T	PLA	Tilbury		1922	69	1960
HL	3530		0-6-0T	PLA	Tilbury		1922	70	1956
HC	1596		0-6-0T	PLA	Royal		1927	71	1959
HC	1597		0-6-0T	PLA	Royal		1927	72	1961
HC	1598		0-6-0T	PLA	Royal		1927	73	1960
P	489		0-4-0ST	PLA	Millwall		1943	74	1958
HC	1719		0-6-0T	PLA	Royal		1943	76	1961
HC	1720		0-6-0T	PLA	Royal		1943	77	1960
MW	1568		0-6-0ST	PLA	Millwall		1943	75	1953
HE	2414		0-6-0ST	PLA	Royal		1943	79	1960
HC	1748		0-6-0ST	PLA	Royal		1944	78	1960

London's Dock Railways: The Royal Docks, North Woolwich and Silvertown

Maker	Works No	Name	Type	Dock Company	Dock Allocated	Running Number	Date Arrived	PLA Number	Date Departed
HE	2876		0-6-0ST	PLA	Royal		1944	80	1960
HE	2881		0-6-0ST	PLA	Royal		1944	81	1959
RSHN	7103		0-6-0ST	PLA	Royal		1944	82	1960
RSHN	7104		0-6-0ST	PLA	Royal		1944	83	1960
RSHN	7105		0-6-0ST	PLA	Royal		1944	84	1959
RSHN	7107		0-6-0ST	PLA	Royal		1944	85	1959
RSHN	7113		0-6-0ST	PLA	Royal		1944	86	1960
HE	2878		0-6-0ST	PLA	Tilbury		1944	87	1960
HE	3166		0-6-0ST	PLA	Tilbury		1944	88	1960
HC	1875		0-4-0ST	PLA	Millwall		1953	89	1963
HC	1873		0-6-0T	PLA	Tilbury		1954	90	1963
HC	1874		0-6-0T	PLA	Tilbury		1954	91	1963
YE	2619		0-6-0DE	PLA	Tilbury		1956	200	1973
YE	2620		0-6-0DE	PLA	Tilbury		1956	201	1972
YE	2630		0-6-0DE	PLA	Tilbury		1956	202	1973
YE	2633		0-6-0DE	PLA	Tilbury		1957	203	1972
YE	2640		0-6-0DE	PLA	Tilbury		1957	204	1972
YE	2641		0-6-0DE	PLA	Tilbury		1957	205	1970
YE	2690		0-6-0DE	PLA	Royal		1959	206	1970
YE	2691		0-6-0DE	PLA	Royal		1959	207	1970
YE	2739		0-6-0DE	PLA	Royal		1959	208	1971
YE	2740		0-6-0DE	PLA	Royal		1959	209	1971
YE	2758		0-6-0DE	PLA	Royal		1959	233	1971
YE	2759		0-6-0DE	PLA	Royal		1959	234	1972
YE	2760		0-6-0DE	PLA	Royal		1959	235	1971
YE	2761		0-6-0DE	PLA	Royal		1959	236	1973
YE	2762		0-6-0DE	PLA	Royal		1959	237	1971
YE	2763		0-6-0DE	PLA	Royal		1959	238	1971
YE	2769		0-6-0DE	PLA	Royal		1960	239	1973
YE	2770		0-6-0DE	PLA	Royal		1960	240	1972
YE	2755		0-6-0DE	PLA	Tilbury		1959	230	1971
YE	2756		0-6-0DE	PLA	Tilbury		1959	231	1973
YE	2757		0-6-0DE	PLA	Tilbury		1959	232	1973
YE	2853		0-4-0DE	PLA	Millwall		1961	210	1971
YE	2854		0-4-0DE	PLA	Millwall		1961	211	1973
YE	2855		0-4-0DE	PLA	Millwall		1961	212	1971
YE	2856		0-4-0DE	PLA	Millwall		1961	213	1971
YE	2857		0-4-0DE	PLA	Millwall		1961	214	1970
YE	2858		0-4-0DE	PLA	Millwall		1961	215	1971

MD	Millwall Dock Company
L&StKD	London & St Katharine Dock Company
E&WID	East & West India Dock Company
L&IDJC	London & India Docks Joint Committee
L&ID	London & India Docks Company
PLA	Port of London Authority
MER	Millwall Extension Railway

CHAPTER 5

The Royal Albert Dock Passenger Railway

The various enclosed docks had been built on bleak, sparsely inhabited marshes away from London's urban sprawl which would take some decades to spread to the East End. In the meantime, labour had to be transported out from the city areas and the dock companies sought various ways to achieve this, in some cases, providing their own passenger railway services. In general terms, legislation governed the fares and frequency of trains to make them convenient and affordable. Thus, many of the dock passenger railways were referred to as "Penny Puffers".

With the building of the Royal Albert Dock, the London and St Katharine Dock Company was authorised to build a railway along its northern boundary to convey passengers and parcels to its steamer terminal at Gallions Reach. The new line connected to the Great Eastern Railway's North Woolwich branch at Albert Dock Junction and a passenger service for *"artisans, mechanics and daily labourers"* operated from Custom House to Gallions, a total of one mile and 61 chains (one and three quarter miles), with intermediate stations at Connaught Road, Central and Manor Way.

The first section of the line opened on 3rd August 1880 and ran from Custom House to Central Station operating a half hourly service between 8.30am and 6pm. The section between Connaught Road and Central was initially single track but this was doubled on 14th November 1881 when the frequency increased to three trains an hour and a full service operated from Custom House to Gallions. The remaining single track from Central to Gallions had opened in October 1880 and was doubled on 1st April 1882.

The line was operated by the dock company who, it is thought, initially used the contractors locomotives

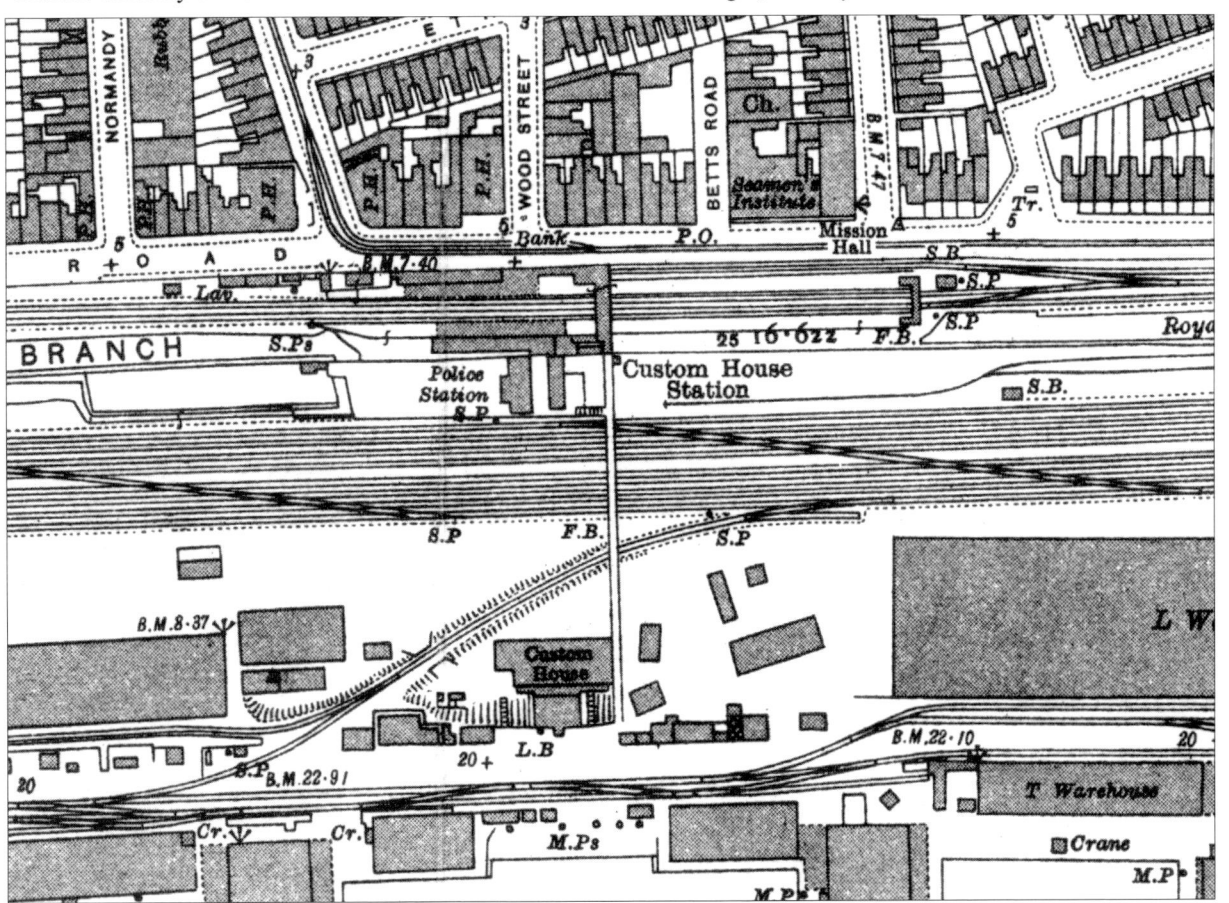

Custom House Station in 1914 with the main line of the North Woolwich Railway spanned by a footbridge. The bay platform on its northern side served as the western terminus of the Royal Albert Dock Railway. The massed sidings across the centre of the map are those of the dock railway. (Crown copyright)

London's Dock Railways: The Royal Docks, North Woolwich and Silvertown

Chelsea and *Long Wind* on hire from Lucas & Aird who had built the dock, but the L&StKD Co subsequently purchased three second-hand locomotives with rolling stock from the London & North Western Railway in 1881. These were previously tender engines converted to 2-4-0 tanks and had already seen around thirty years service by the time they began work at the docks. The locos had cylinders of 15in x 20in with 5ft 0in driving wheels and were given a new green livery with black and yellow lining. They had "Royal Albert Dock" emblazoned on their side tanks. Their previous nameplates of *President, John O'Gaunt* and *Hercules*, were retained but had been hidden behind the side tanks after conversion.

The company hired a bay platform at Custom House and, as with its other stations, employed its own staff for operation of the line and issue of tickets. These were initially a penny for third class travel, rising to three pence for a first class fare. From July 1881 the Great Eastern Railway also began running hourly through trains from Fenchurch Street to Gallions but fares on non dock company trains were subject to additional charges per mile.

By 1896 the three ex-LNWR engines were nearing their half century and considered no longer serviceable and, under the administration of the London & India Docks Joint Committee, they were withdrawn from service on the 1st July that year. They then performed the odd shunting duties before being sold for scrap to George Cohen Sons & Co Ltd of Canning Town a month later. The local service from Custom House to Gallions was then taken over by the GER who used their own engines and rolling stock but dock company employees continued to man the stations, signal boxes and crossings.

By 1900, the line had reached its peak when over 50 trains ran each way on weekdays with thirteen running direct from Fenchurch Street and Stratford to Gallions. At times during that period the railway saw the occasional dock company loco used as a spare engine and, around 1903, the former L&StKD Co Fox Walker No 263 was fitted with brackets for destination boards for use there. RS No 3050 *Looe* is also recorded as working the line.

Above: An LNER train for Albert Docks headed by loco No 7189 at Custom House Station in 1939. The disused bay platform for the Albert Dock line can be seen on the right. (Jim Peden Collection/Industrial Railway Society)

Opposite: The mock Tudor main building at Connaught Road Station c1939. The line in the distance leading off to the left is the branch to North Woolwich. (Jim Peden Collection/Industrial Railway Society)

The Royal Albert Dock Passenger Railway

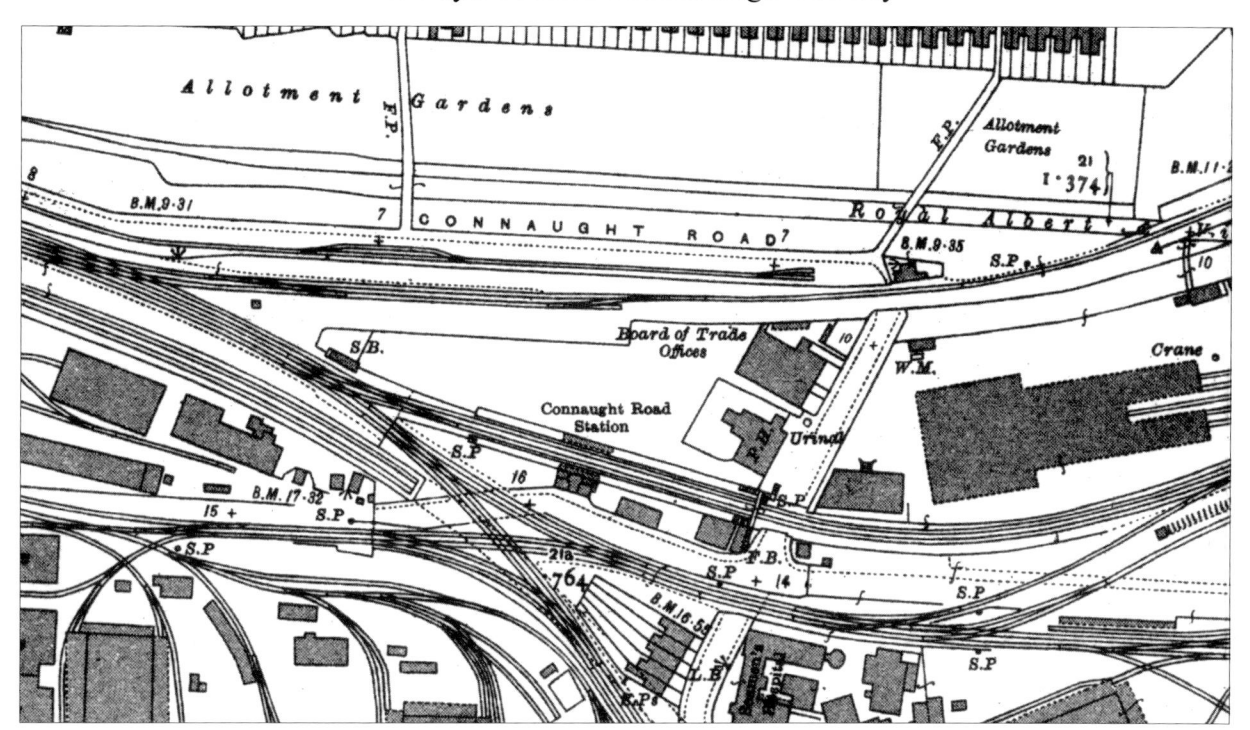

The junction at Connaught Road Station showing the twin tracks of the Royal Albert Dock Railway and the North Woolwich line branching off to the bottom of the map. The line to the north of the Board of Trade offices heads off to Beckton. (Crown Copyright)

London's Dock Railways: The Royal Docks, North Woolwich and Silvertown

Connaught Road Station was the first stop from Custom House on the Royal Albert Dock line. Situated 220 yards east of Albert Dock Junction it was opened on 3rd of August 1880 but did not appear on the timetables until November that year. Its main building on the up side was in mock Tudor style.

The next station, Central, was built at the same time and was shown on the timetable as *"terminus of shuttle from Custom House"* until the line was extended to Manor Way station in July 1881.

Manor Way station had originally been named Manor Road but, in any case, it remained in place only until 1886 when it was rebuilt on the opposite side of the street. Due to road widening it underwent yet another change in 1926 when it was enlarged, but lost its street level signal box. The down platform at Manor Way was demolished soon after closure in 1940 but the up platform remained until the 1980s as the street level buildings had been converted into two commercial properties, one as a post office. The station was sited in a cutting which has since been filled in and no traces remain.

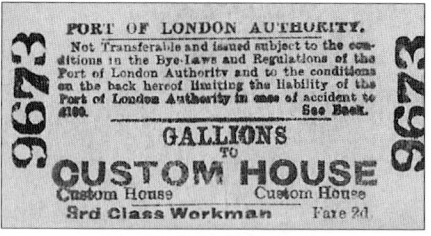

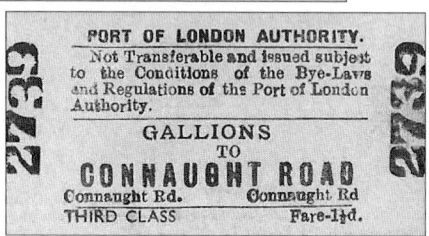

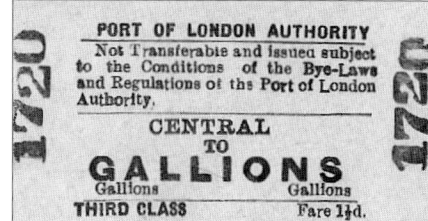

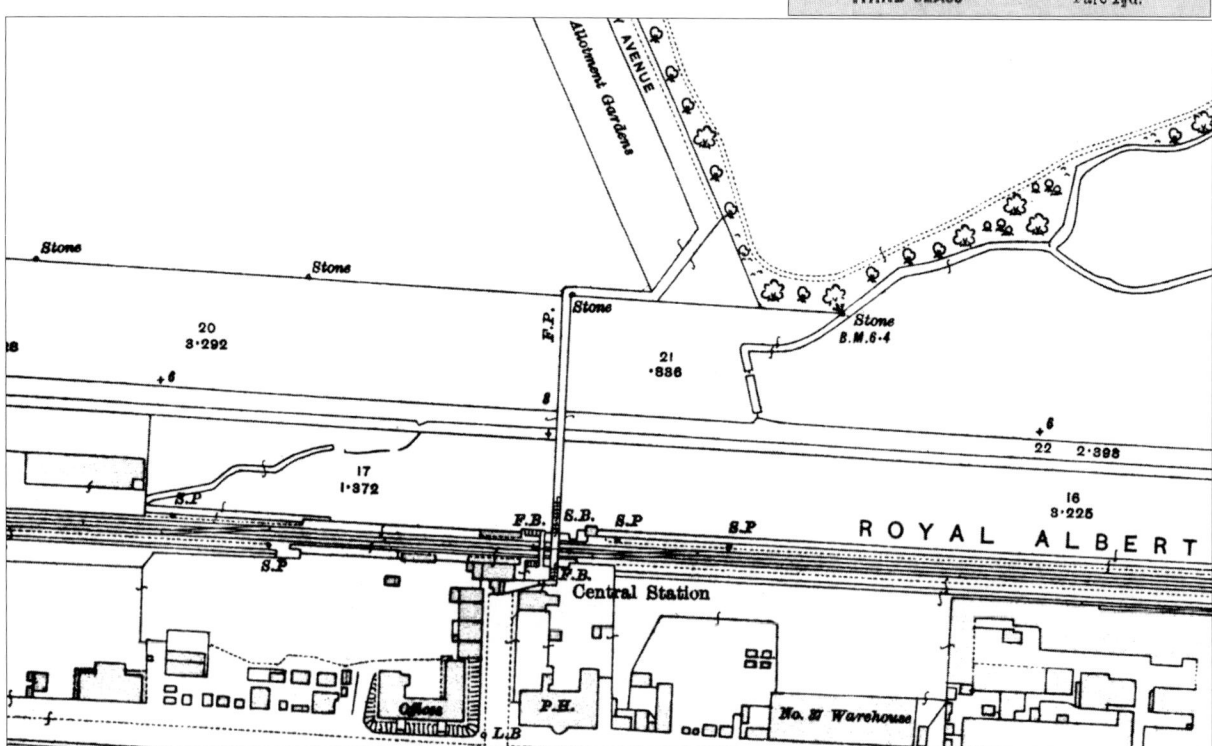

Above: *Central Station was halfway along the Royal Albert Dock but still in a fairly isolated area in 1894. (Crown Copyright)*

Opposite: *LNER Loco No 7142 with a train for the Albert Dock at Manor Way Station in 1939. (Jim Peden Collection/Industrial Railway Society)*

The Royal Albert Dock Passenger Railway

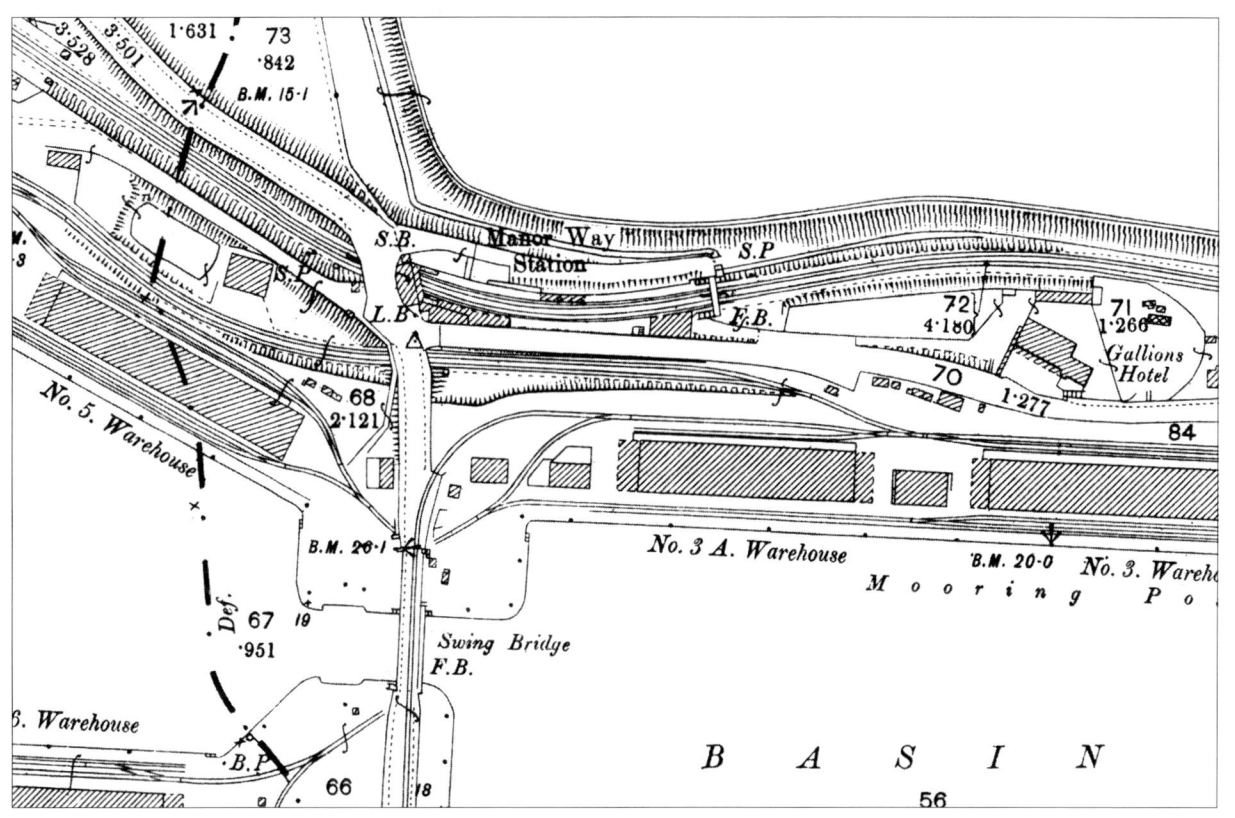

Manor Way station was just a short distance from the original terminus at the Gallions Hotel seen at the far right in 1894. (Crown Copyright)

London's Dock Railways: The Royal Docks, North Woolwich and Silvertown

The "new" Gallions Station was built in 1886 and Royal Albert Dock loco No 7 was pictured there with a train of seven four-wheeler coaches bound for Custom House around 1890. (John Alsop Collection)

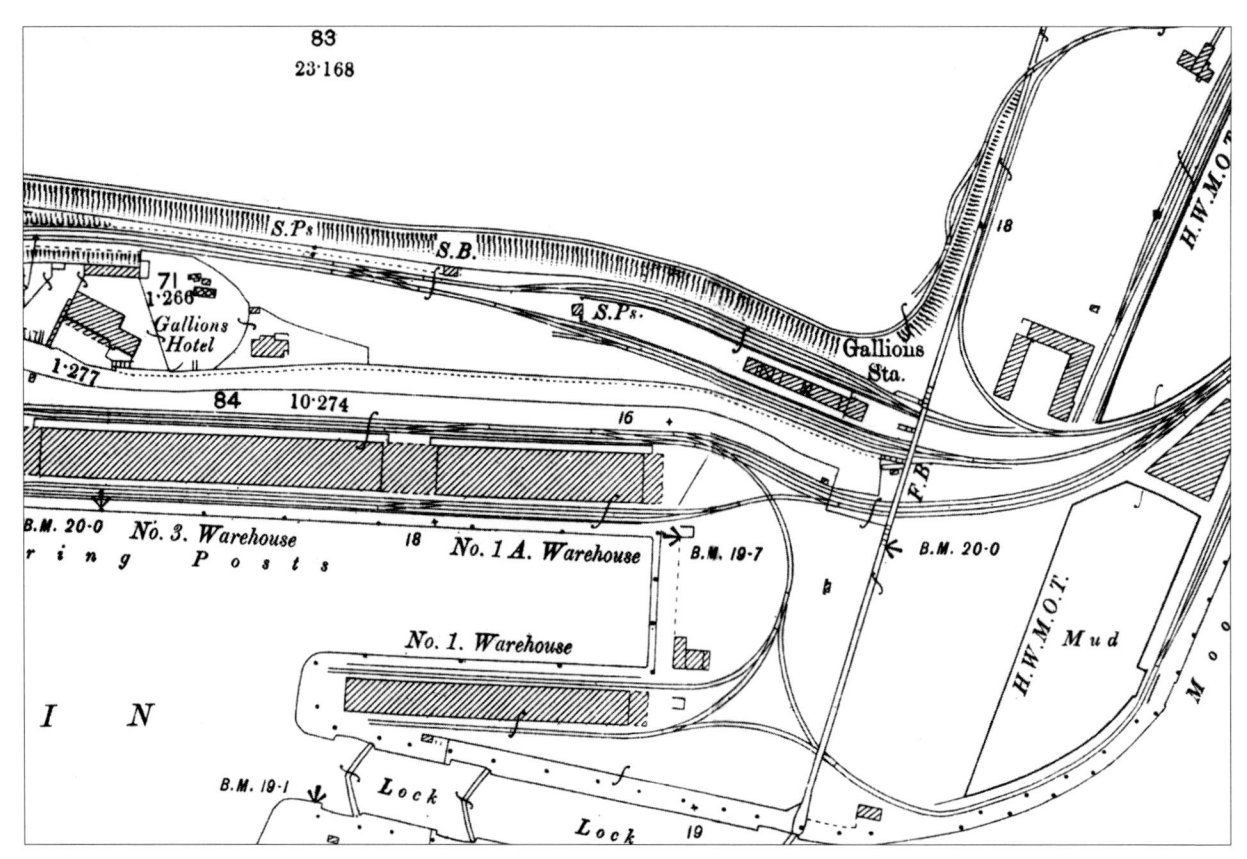

An 1894 map showing the western end of the Royal Albert Dock Railway with its terminus at Gallions Station. The Gallions Hotel that marked the former terminus can be seen at the left centre. The tracks at the far right lead to the coaling jetties of Cory & Son. (Crown Copyright)

92

The Royal Albert Dock Passenger Railway

Almost the end of Manor Way station where the up platform buildings survived after closure when converted to shops. They were derelict when this photo was taken in 1978 and finally demolished a few years afterwards. (Tony Harden)

Another photo of loco No 7 at the later Gallions station with a Custom House train. (Author's Collection)

London's Dock Railways: The Royal Docks, North Woolwich and Silvertown

The original station at Gallions opened on 30th October 1880 when only one train per day ran in each direction. The station and had an integral hotel, whereby its main doors opened out onto the platform. Travellers could stay at the hotel while awaiting their steamer departure at Gallions Reach. Alterations to the Albert Dock entrance lock necessitated a realignment of the track and a new station was built nearer the river some 275 yards further to the east of the hotel in December 1886. The new Gallions station had an island platform with GER trains using the north platform (No 1) and the dock company's shuttle occupying the south platform (No 2). The "new" Gallions station underwent a number changes when the original platform and buildings were altered in 1925.

Gallions station marked the end of the Royal Albert Dock Passenger railway, but that was not the end of the line as a branch continued to a coal wharf where sidings served a 500 yard long jetty which was opened in 1886. A number of coal companies had amalgamated in 1896 to form William Cory & Son and, at its height, the firm handled some five millions tons of fuel

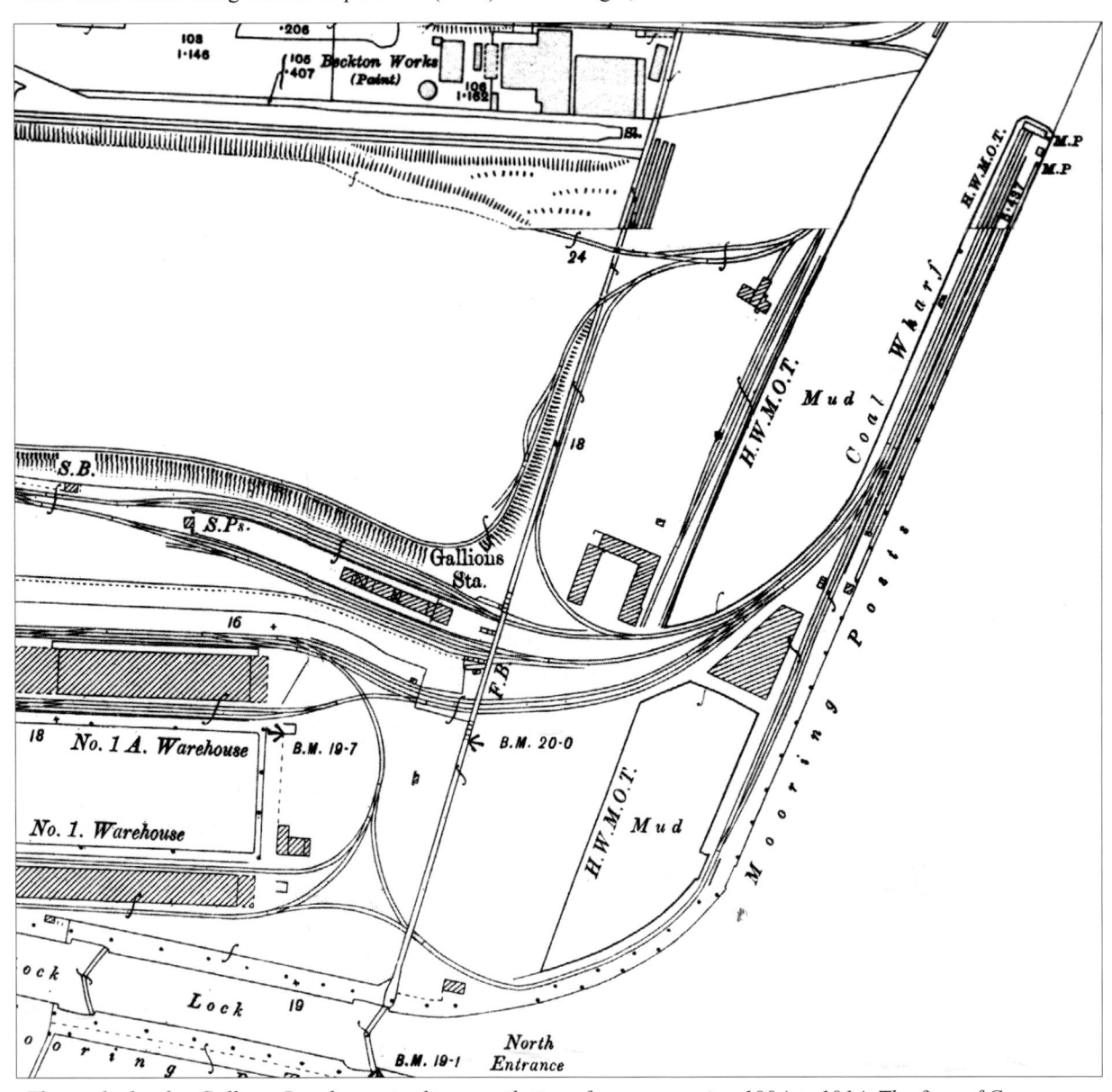

The coal wharf at Gallions Reach seen in this compilation of maps spanning 1894 to 1914. The firm of Cory Brothers operated the system from 1896 until its closure in 1967. (Crown Copyright)

The Royal Albert Dock Passenger Railway

per year for the industrial and domestic London market. Cory's had their own locomotives which totalled 13 during their years of operation that ended in 1967. They were:

AP	4wWT	No 3888/1897	*Belvedere*
AE	0-4-0ST	No 1578/1910	*Jetty*
BH	0-4-0ST	No 1038/1893	*Deptford*
S	4wVBT	No 7060/1927	*Woolwich*
S	4wVBT	No 7696/1929	*Greenwich*
S	4wVBT	No 8796/1933	*Charlton*
S	4wVBT	No 9365/1945	*Belvedere*
JF	0-4-0DM	No 19351/1931	*Oberon*
JF	0-4-0DM	No 19024/1930	*Circe*
VF	0-4-0DM	No D98/1949	*Perseus*
VF	0-4-0DM	No D99/1949	*Pegasus*
VF	0-4-0DM	No D293/1955	*Priam*
VF	0-4-0DM	No D294/1955	*Teucer*

Services on the Royal Albert Dock Passenger Railway had been considerably reduced during World War One, with Sunday timetables suspended from June 1915 and bank holiday trains axed from early 1918. Towards the latter part of the conflict the railway ran special trains for munitions workers who were transported from Gallions across the Thames to Woolwich Arsenal, but after the war ended passenger numbers declined further and never recovered to earlier levels. By 6th June 1932 the local service between Custom House and Gallions had been suspended, although through trains continued to run, but by October 1939 the frequency had dropped to just half the 1900 peak of 53 trains each way on weekdays, with no trains at all between Saturday lunchtimes and Monday mornings.

The line to Gallions finally ceased operation after a World War Two air raid on 7th September 1940. The bomb-damaged tracks were given minimal repairs for wagon storage but the passenger service was never resumed and the line was officially abandoned in 1950.

Gallions station was a hive of activity when this photo was taken around 1930, when William Cory & Son had two Sentinel locomotives, "Woolwich" and "Greenwich", one of which is in the foreground, the other in the distance at the top left of the picture. LNER locomotives and passenger stock complete the scene. (Colin Withey Collection)

London's Dock Railways: The Royal Docks, North Woolwich and Silvertown

The Cory Brothers Terminal at Gallions Reach seen here in September 1968. Rail traffic had ceased in the previous year but VF shunter No D294 "Teucer" remained on site before being sold shortly after this photo was taken. (Nick Catford)

Gallions station, seen here in 1939, had very little future as a passenger terminus after bombs fell on the line during the following year. (Jim Peden Collection/Industrial Railway Society)

The Royal Albert Dock Passenger Railway

Although the line to Gallions had closed, Custom House station remained in operation while serving the North Woolwich Branch (see that chapter) which closed on the 9th December 2006, having undergone several alterations and "modernisations" in the meantime. However, the station's future is assured through becoming incorporated into the Docklands Light Railway. Elsewhere, the former Gallions Hotel still stands. It was in use as a public house until 1972 and then stood derelict for many years as a Grade II listed building until a recent redevelopment of the area and the building has now been refurbished for housing.

Looking west from the site of the former Gallions station on 5th May 1965. The former Gallions Hotel stands on the left of the picture with the remains of Manor Way station in the distance. (A E Bennett/Transport Treasury)

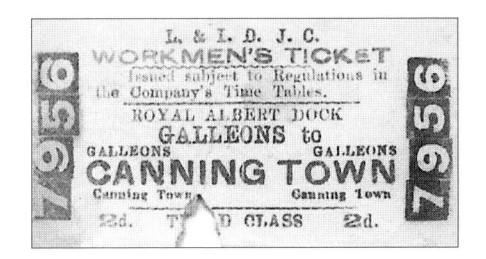

London's Dock Railways: The Royal Docks, North Woolwich and Silvertown

The dilapidated former Gallions Hotel in 1980 with a section of the original station platform still in place. (Nick Catford)

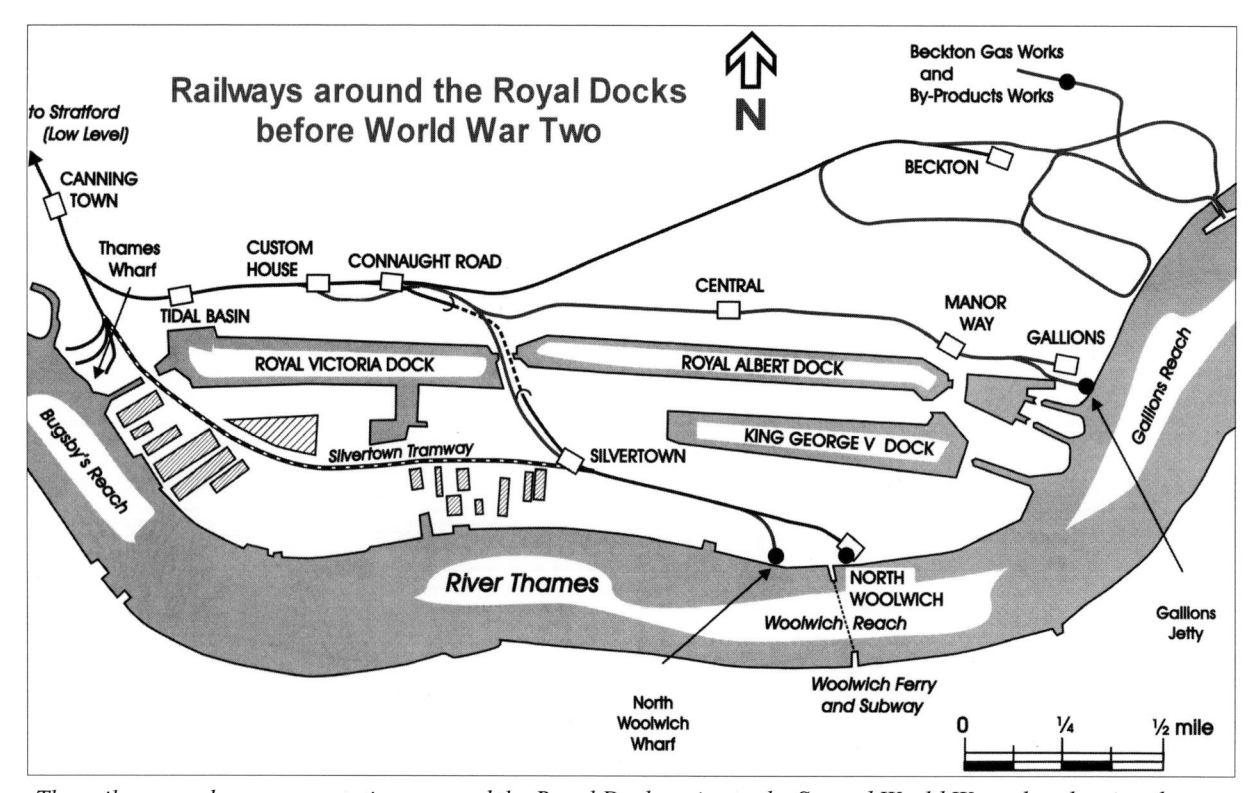

The railways and passenger stations around the Royal Docks prior to the Second World War, also showing the branch to Beckton and its gasworks. (Map by Roger Hateley)

The Royal Albert Dock Passenger Railway

London & St Katharine Dock Company 2-4-0T ex-L&NWR No 1819

Name:	*(President)*
Manufacturer:	Crewe Works
Built:	1850
Running number:	5 (L&StKD Co and L&IDJC), 238 and 1819 (both L&NWR)
At the Docks:	1881–1896

Originally a 2-4-0 tender engine named *President*, this loco was built as No 238 by the London & North West Railway Company in May 1850. In March 1871 it was rebuilt as a 2-4-0 tank and renumbered 1819 before being purchased by the dock Company in April 1881, along with two sister engines, numbers 1911 and 1927. Given the number 5 it operated the service to Gallions with the other two until being withdrawn in July 1896 and sold for scrap to the firm of George Cohen at nearby Canning Town in August 1896.

London & St Katharine Dock Company 2-4-0T ex-L&NWR No 1927

Name:	*(John O'Gaunt)*
Manufacturer:	Crewe Works
Built:	1849
Running number:	6 (L&StKD Co and L&IDJC), 250 and 1927 (both L&NWR)
At the Docks:	1881–1896

The second of a trio of second hand locomotives built by the London & North Western Railway in November 1849 and purchased by the L&StKD Co to operate the services to Gallions. Like the others, this started life as a 2-4-0 tender engine numbered 250 and was named *John O'Gaunt* before conversion to tank form in December 1860 and being renumbered 1927. Having arrived at Custom House with the others in April 1881 it was numbered 6 and remained until all three were sold to George Cohen at Canning Town for scrap in August 1896.

A rare glimpse of the Albert Dock No 6 at Custom House station in 1890 under the administration of the London & India Dock Joint Committee. (Author's Collection)

London & St Katharine Docks Company 2-4-0T ex-L&NWR No 1911

Name: (Marquis), (Hercules)

Manufacturer: Crewe Works

Built: 1847

Running number: 7 (L&StKD Co and L&IDJC), 102, 431 and 1911 (all LNWR)

At the Docks: 1881–1896

Last of three former London & North Western 2-4-0 tender engines to find their way to the Royal Docks for use on the Gallions railway by the L&StKD Co. Built in March 1847 it was originally numbered 102 and named *Marquis* by the L&NWR but was renumbered 431 when rebuilt as a 2-4-0 tank in May 1859 and renamed *Hercules* in 1864, having been renumbered once again to 1911. After being sold to the L&StKD Co in April 1881 it ran as dock company No 7 until sold for scrap in August 1896 to dealers George Cohen at Canning Town.

Ex LNWR No 1911 running as No 7 on the Gallions branch line. (Bert Moody Collection)

CHAPTER 6

The North Woolwich Railway

The Eastern Counties and Thames Junction Railway was opened from Stratford to Barking Road (Canning Town) on 29th April 1846 and, in the meantime, an act of 1845 enabled a branch to North Woolwich to be completed and purchased by the Eastern Counties Railway on 14th June 1847. An hourly service then ran from Stratford to the Thames where a steam ferry service, also operated by the railway company, provided links across to Woolwich, predominantly used by munitions workers at the Arsenal. At that time Woolwich itself had no railway connection and ferries were a vital link across the river. The passenger service suffered a decline after the South Eastern Railway had opened its line to Woolwich on the south side of the river in 1849, although some urbanisation around the North Woolwich terminus had improved matters.

During the building of the Victoria Dock the line encountered difficulties as it crossed the entrance lock near Bow Creek, where a swing bridge created problems for both rail and shipping movements. To solve this predicament, the railway was rerouted along the north and east of the dock and the new line was completed by the time the dock opened in 1855, when a new station was also provided at Custom House.

The revised route rejoined its original tracks at a new junction, which became known as Silvertown, three quarters of a mile from the terminus. The southern course of the original railway was then referred to as the "Woolwich Abandoned Line" which came under the Victoria Dock Company ownership and continued to operate until fairly recent times as the Silvertown Tramway (see that chapter), serving a multitude of in-

Heavy traffic in the 1920s on the level crossing at Victoria Dock Road west of Tidal Basin Station near the junction of North Woolwich Road and Tidal Basin Road. The lines branching off to the left lead to the Thames Wharf sidings. (Island History Trust)

London's Dock Railways: The Royal Docks, North Woolwich and Silvertown

Despite sustaining substantial bomb damage Tidal Basin station remained open during most of the war years but falling passenger numbers brought about closure in 1943. (Author's Collection)

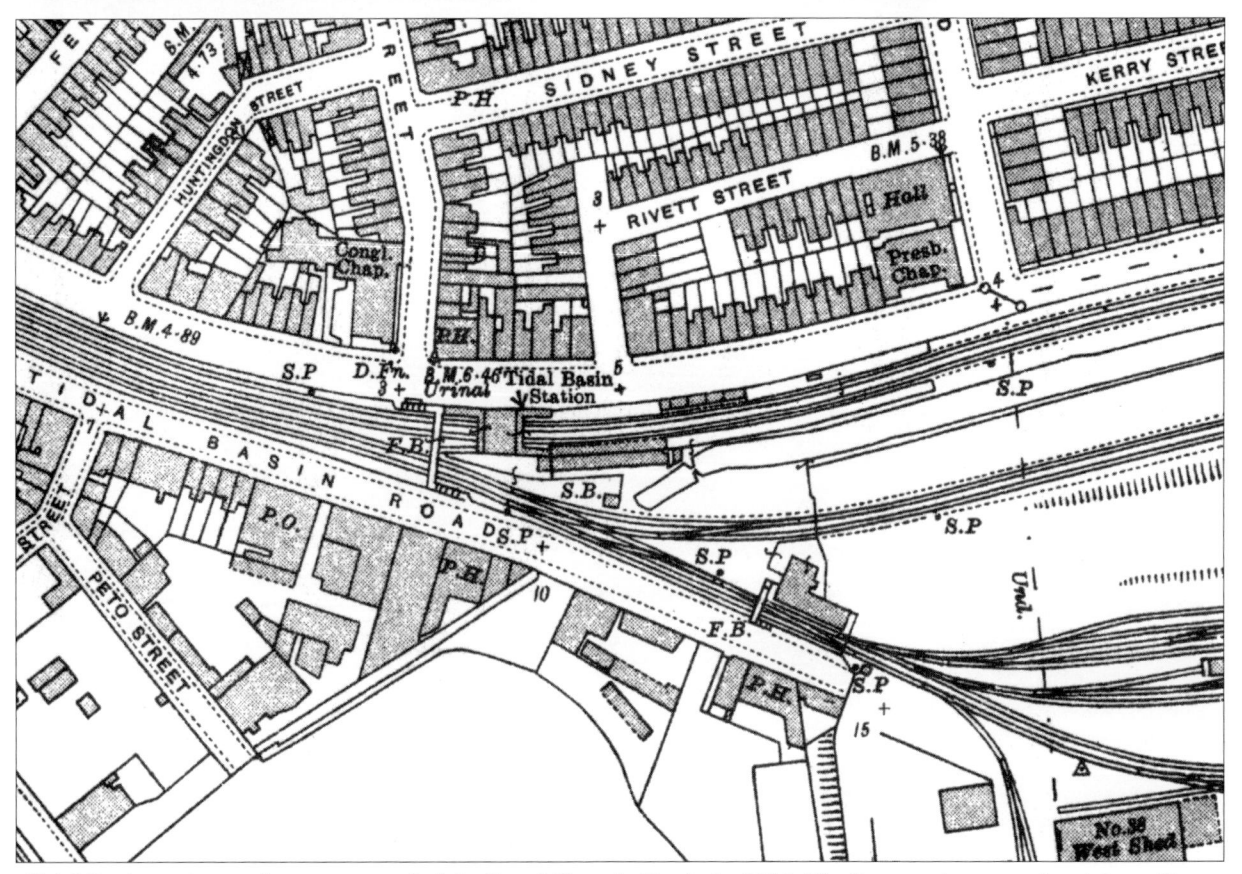

Tidal Basin station at the western end of the Royal Victoria Docks in 1914. The line continues on the right to Custom House (Crown Copyright)

The North Woolwich Railway

dustrial premises along its route. A new station at Tidal Basin, alternatively known as Victoria Dock station, was built in 1858 at the western end of the dock.

In 1852 the firm of S W Silver & Company had established a large factory with a connection to the original railway. The works were adjacent to the junction of the old and new lines where a station was built, appropriately named Silvertown after the local benefactors. It opened in 19th June 1863 under the Great Eastern Railway.

The revised route then suffered more upheaval with plans for further development to the east of Victoria Dock. The proposed Albert Dock would be connected to the Victoria Dock by means of a short canal which would, once again, cut across the route of the railway. The solution was to build a tunnel beneath it and this, the Connaught Tunnel, was completed in 1878.

The high level route was retained via a swing bridge while the tunnel ran for 600 yards under the cut and tracks were laid some 23 feet below the low water mark. On either side of the tunnel a gradient of 1 in 50 ran through open cuttings up to ground level. The ninety feet span swing bridge for road and rail was built across the canal and this section of line came under the ownership of the dock company, which was also responsible for maintenance of the tunnel and the retaining walls on either side of the cuttings. Henceforth, the railway company was charged a toll per goods or passenger vehicles for any use of the high level crossing. Goods trains through the tunnel were limited to 25 wagons with strict instructions relating to brakes and the tensions of couplings. In the event of the tunnel being out of use for any time the GER maintained the right to use the high level route free of charge.

The timber built Silvertown Station looking eastwards towards North Woolwich around 1910. The former works of S W Silver & Co can be seen on the right. (John Alsop Collection)

London's Dock Railways: The Royal Docks, North Woolwich and Silvertown

The Great Eastern Railway's ferry "Middlesex" sets off from Woolwich pier on its last day of operation on 30th September 1908. (John Alsop Collection)

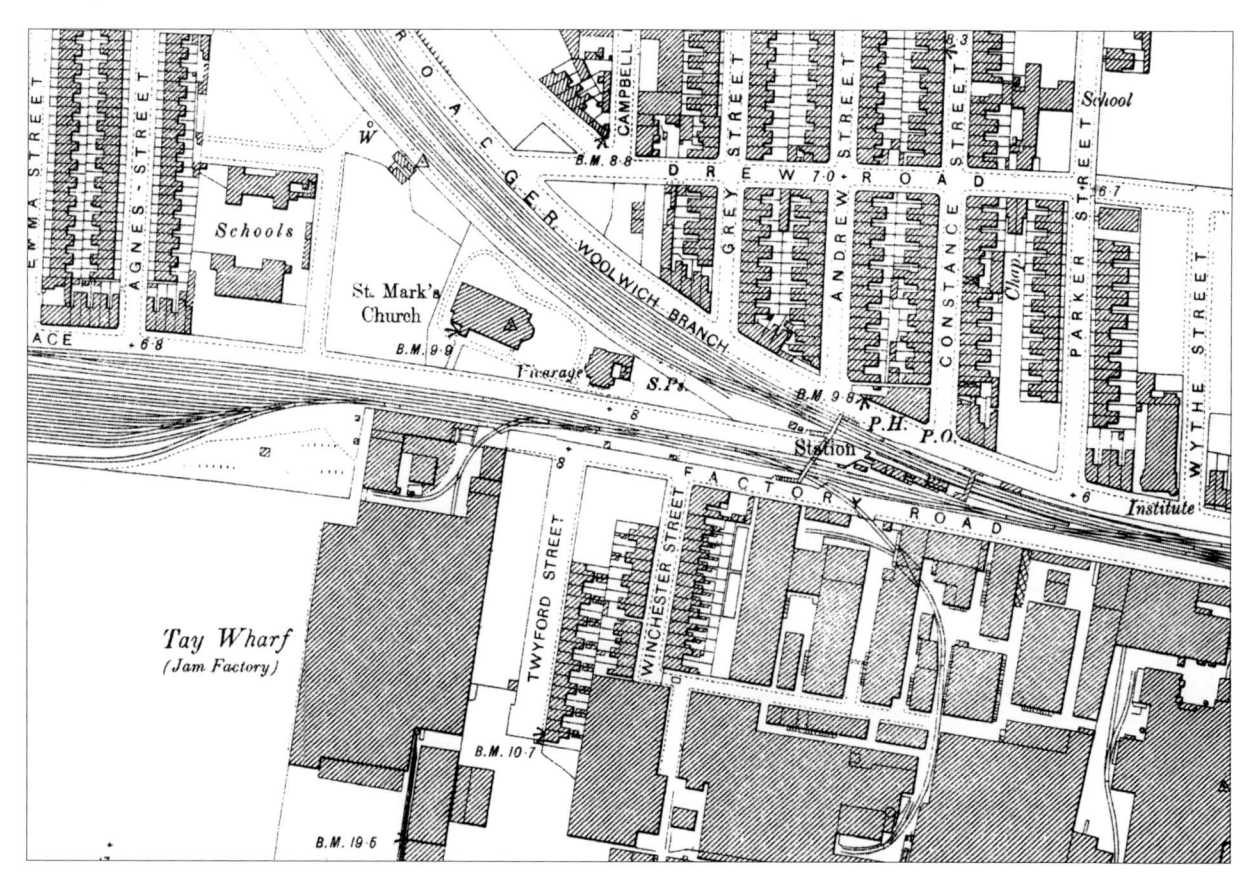

The old and new routes converge at Silvertown junction on the 1894 map. Silver's works are at the bottom right along Factory Road. The "abandoned" line across the left centre still had plenty of traffic to feed the sidings of the numerous factories. (Crown Copyright)

The North Woolwich Railway

The section of the railway between Silvertown Junction and North Woolwich had sidings into various industrial concerns. Tate & Lyle's Thames Sugar Refinery (see the chapter on the Silvertown Tramway) had their own locomotive but the adjacent Silvertown Gasworks relied on the GER for shunting its traffic. The works was built in 1864 by the Victoria Docks Gas Company for the supply of gas to East Ham, the County Borough of West Ham and later to parts of Essex after its take-over by the GLCC. It had sidings around the works and down to the riverside. Gas production ceased in September 1909 when supplies were taken over by the huge neighbouring Beckton works.

To the west of the terminus, North Woolwich Wharf was originally occupied by W T Henley & Co who made submarine cables, and the firm of William Griffiths & Co took over the site to handle quarried stone and sought permission for a siding connected to the North Woolwich Railway on 11th June 1889. Three locomotives were employed there over a period from 1900 until the works closed in 1939. They were:

TG   0-4-0ST No 227/1900 *Ida*
HE   0-4-0ST No 620/1895 *Joe*
MW 0-4-0PM No 1951/1918

On 23rd March 1889 the Woolwich Free Ferry was opened by the Metropolitan Board of Works and became a cheaper alternative to the through ticketing offered by the railway, whose own ferry service finally closed on 30th September 1908. Meanwhile, Tidal Dock station was rebuilt in 1893 and, due to lack of space at the site, the booking office was integrated with a footbridge over the tracks.

Improvements to, and the deepening of, the Royal Victoria and Albert Docks from 1936 found the North Woolwich line to be an impedance to plans once again. Larger vessels required a deeper and wider passage between the two docks with the problem being how to deepen the Connaught Cutting without damaging the tunnel below it. This was achieved by reducing the tunnel's height and width by lining it with rings of steel segments rather like the London Underground and this allowed the base of the cutting to be lowered by three feet.

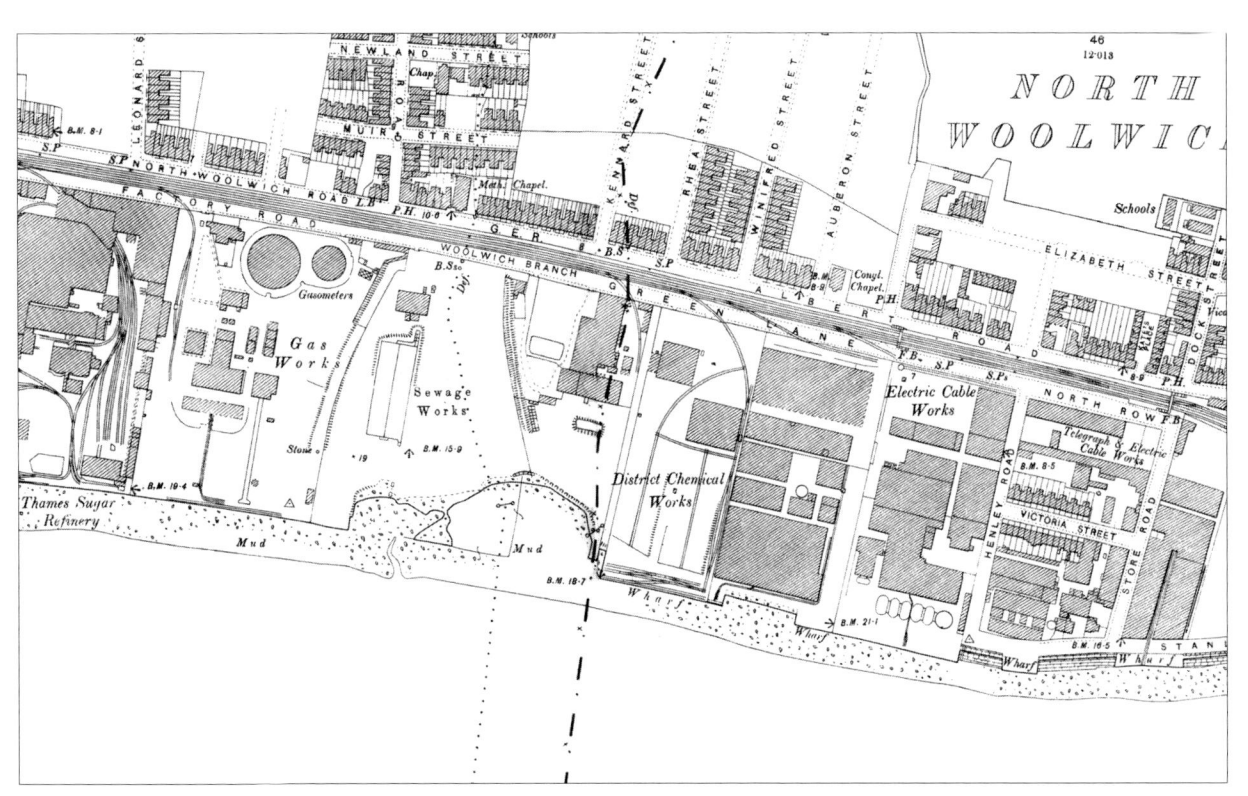

This section of the North Woolwich Railway between Silvertown Junction and its terminus shows connections to the Thames Sugar Refinery, Silvertown Gasworks and Griffiths' premises on the site of the cable works at North Woolwich Wharf in 1894. (Crown copyright)

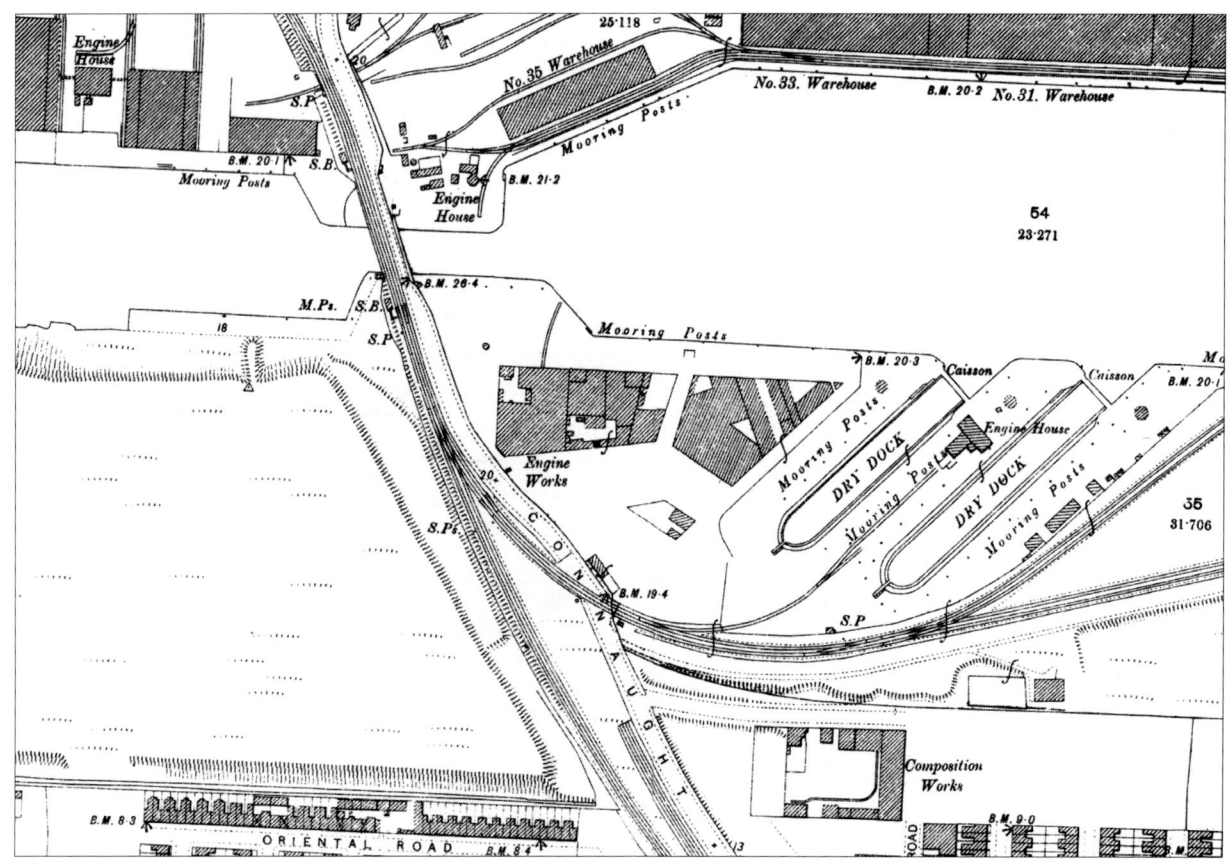

A section of the North Woolwich line runs above and below the Connaught Passage between the Victoria and Albert Docks in 1894. (Crown Copyright)

The North Woolwich Railway

During the Second World War enemy action had closed the branch from Custom House to Gallions and the North Woolwich line also fell victim to bombing. Tidal Basin was briefly closed after being damaged on 29th March 1941 but then reopened despite seeing very few passengers and, after numbers dwindled even further, it closed for good on 15th August 1943. The stations at Custom House and North Woolwich had also both been struck during the blitz on 7th September 1940, the terminus suffering considerable damage to its buildings and canopies along with a train that was standing there.

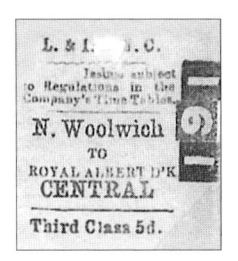

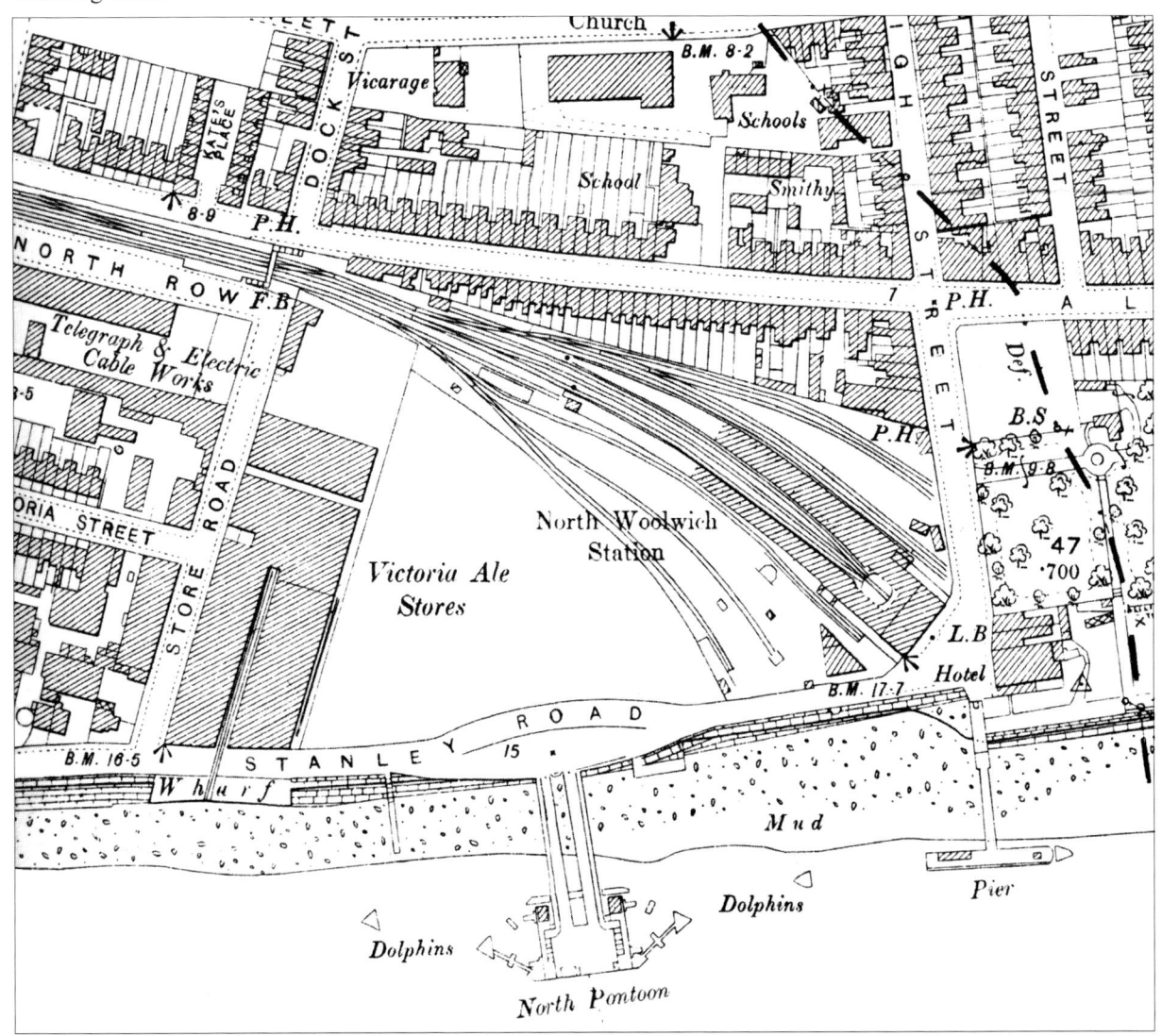

Above: *The terminus at North Woolwich in 1894 with the railway ferry pier at the bottom right and the relatively new pontoon for the Free Ferry adjacent. (Crown copyright)*
Opposite: *The scene at North Woolwich Station looking south towards the Thames in August 1912. (John Alsop Collection)*

Inside the Connaught tunnel showing the steel segment lining that reduced its height allowing the cutting above to be deepened. (Courtesy of Crossrail Ltd)

Looking north across the Connaught swing bridge on 25th March 1961. (A E Bennett/Transport Treasury)

The North Woolwich Railway

BR No 69668 heads down towards the south portal of the Connaught Tunnel with a train from Silvertown to Stratford on 25th March 1961. (A E Bennett/ Transport Treasury)

A train from Silvertown descends to the Connaught Tunnel as BR No 69724 passes St Mark's Church on 29th April 1961. (A E Bennett/Transport Treasury)

London's Dock Railways: The Royal Docks, North Woolwich and Silvertown

In later years, buses, trolley buses and road haulage all took their toll on the railway. Passenger services from Custom House to the terminus were expected to close in 1970 but they were subject to a reprieve after a joint initiative between the Greater London Council and British Rail, which saw a revised new timetable from North Woolwich to Stratford. With the exception of the long abandoned Tidal Basin, all the stations along the route were rebuilt and the line reduced to a single track, with the single platforms having their buildings replaced by minimal shelters.

During the 1970s and 1980s part of the North Woolwich terminus goods yard was used as a scrap metal depot under several names including that of the Steel & Alloy Scrap Company. Several locomotives had been sent there for breaking up and among those noted were:

FH 4WDM   No 3641/1953
RH 4wDM   No 476142/1953 *Bounty*
RH 0-4-0DE No 416211/1957 *Hornblower*

Despite the reprieve, the line eventually closed on 9th December 2006 after the new stopping points on the Docklands Light Railway at North Woolwich and Silvertown came within close proximity of the original stations. The old terminus building at North Woolwich was refurbished as a museum in November 1984 and in its time housed nine locomotives but the venture failed and all were dispersed to other locations. The locos were:

N   0-4-0ST No 2119/1876
MW   0-6-0ST No 1317/1895 *Rhiwnant*
MW   0-6-0ST No 1762/1910 *Dolobran*
MW   0-6-0ST No 2009/1921 *Rhyl*
MW   0-6-0ST No 2015/1921 *Abernant*
AE   0-6-0ST No 2068/1933
P   0-6-0ST No 2000/1942
FH   4wDM   No 3294/1948 *Barking Power Dudley*
RSH 0-6-0ST No 7667/1950

It was also hoped to restore a section of the line as a heritage railway but the funding was never raised and the site was eventually earmarked for redevelopment with the main building's future undecided. However, the line itself has not died completely as plans are in progress to incorporate a section of it, along with the Connaught Tunnel, as part of the new Crossrail route through London. During this work the tunnel will be enlarged by the 'cut and cover' method, exposing the tracks for the first time since they were laid in 1878.

The former Kent & East Sussex Railway No 29 (RSH No 7667) pictured at the old North Woolwich Station on 3rd December 1985. (Ken Scanes)

The North Woolwich Railway

Another of the locos at the ill fated North Woolwich Station Museum was Peckett No 2000, photographed there on 3rd December 1985. (Ken Scanes)

GER loco No 229 (Neilson & Co No 2119) was literally "out in the cold" when photographed at the North Woolwich Station Museum on 20th January 1987. (Ken Scanes)

The tunnel on the disused route under the Connaught Canal as built in 1878. Its restricted dimensions mean it will have to be rebuilt for future traffic. (Courtesy of Crossrail Ltd)

One of the semi derelict tunnel portals in 2010. Trains will return in the near future. (Courtesy of Crossrail Ltd)

CHAPTER 7

The Silvertown Tramway

The former route of the North Woolwich Railway (see that chapter) to the south of the Victoria Dock became known as the "Abandoned Line" but this was far from the case as it continued to serve the many industrial premises along its course. Latterly named the Silvertown Tramway it remained in use until around 1991.

Originally opened in 1847 as the Eastern Counties Railway to North Woolwich, the line between Silvertown and the old swing bridge near Bow Creek came under the ownership of the Victoria Dock Company when the route was diverted around the north and east of the dock in 1855, after which, railway company shunting movements to factories along the original line became liable to charges by the dock company. This proved a valuable source of revenue to the dock company as traffic on this branch was frequent and bountiful. Trains along the tramway were limited to three miles per hour and no loose shunting was permitted on any of the sidings. There were many private sidings connected to the line, with several industries having their own locomotives. Great Eastern Railway (later LNER) engines were rostered to collect and manoeuvre wagons at Silvertown Yard for onward transit through Silvertown station and the railway network beyond the docks.

Most of the premises served by the tramway lined the foreshore of the River Thames and, starting from the Silvertown end of the line, the first major industrial concern was S W Silver's waterproof clothing works. This was established in 1852 and was of such benefit to the locality that a new station there was named after the company. The factory afterwards became the India Rubber, Gutta Percha and Telegraph Works (see map in the North Woolwich Railway chapter).

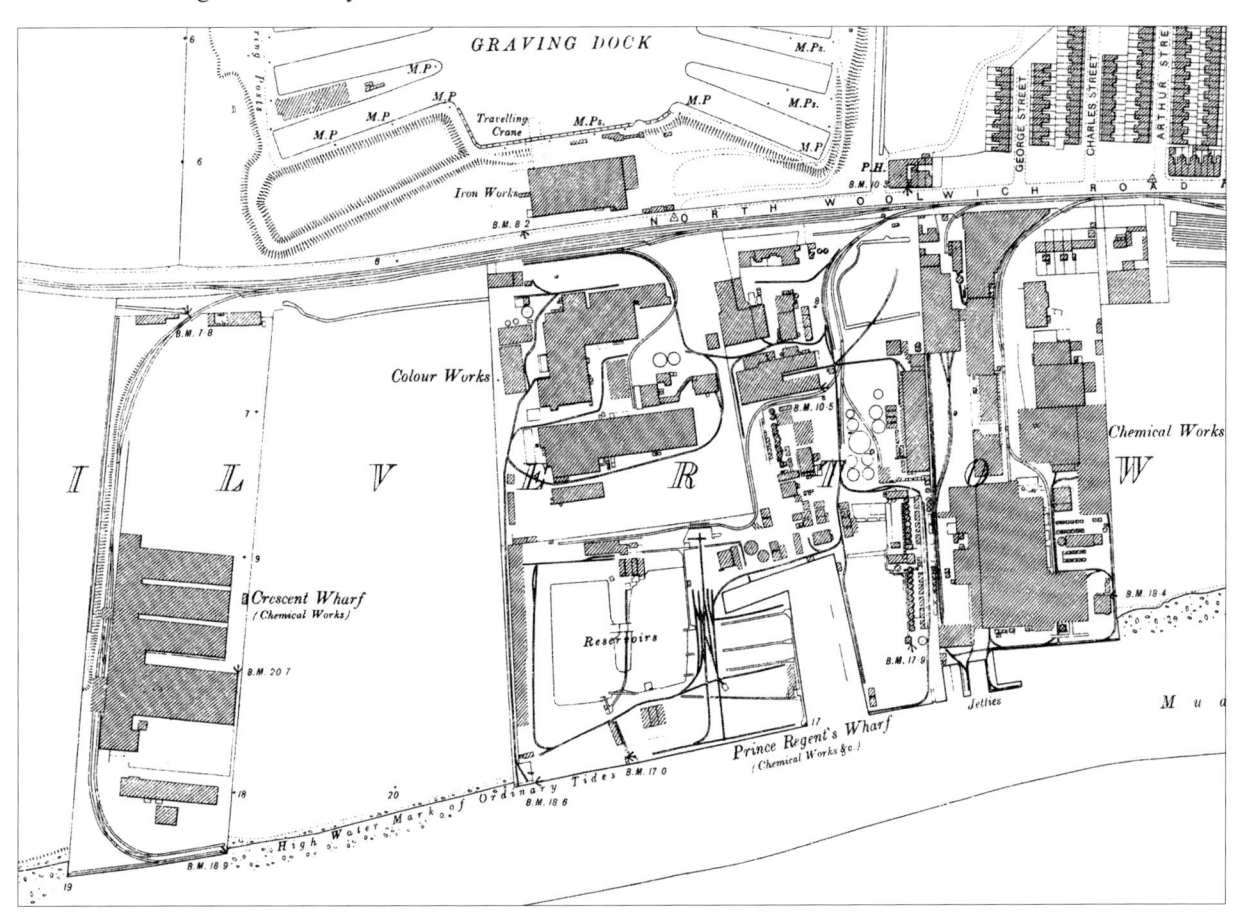

Chemical works abound along the Silvertown Tramway's middle section in 1893. A map of the eastern end can be seen in the North Woolwich Railway chapter. (Crown Copyright)

London's Dock Railways: The Royal Docks, North Woolwich and Silvertown

Next in line was the jam and marmalade factory of James Keiller, established at Tay Wharf in 1880, then came the tar and creosote works of Burt Boulton & Haywood which opened in 1856 and later became the site of the National Radiator Works.

The sugar refinery of Tate & Lyle was established in 1869. They had their own loco in the early part of the 20th century. This was an 0-4-0 saddletank built by Manning Wardle in 1905, works number 1671 and named *Elsie* which came from Burry Port Copper Works in West Wales, possibly at the time when they were advertising for a loco in 1925. This engine worked there until sold for scrap to the nearby firm of Thomas W Ward in 1934.

The Silvertown Flour Mills of the Co-operative Wholesale Society had two locos, both 0-4-0 saddle tanks that were supplied new from Peckett & Sons. The first was No 1114 built in 1907 which worked until sold around March 1928 to London dealers C R Cole and eventually moved on to Dunlop & Co Ltd at Birmingham. Its replacement was No 1739, built in 1928, which lasted until sold to T W Ward in November 1949 and worked at their ship breaking Yard at Inverkeithing in Fife, Scotland. In 1945 the mills were leased to Spillers Ltd whose own premises had been destroyed by bombing in World War II. Spillers built new mills at the nearby Victoria Docks and commenced operations there in January 1953.

Continuing westwards was the scrap yard of Thomas W Ward Ltd whose premises were home to at least 15 locomotives between 1907 and 1991, not to mention many others that ended their days there under

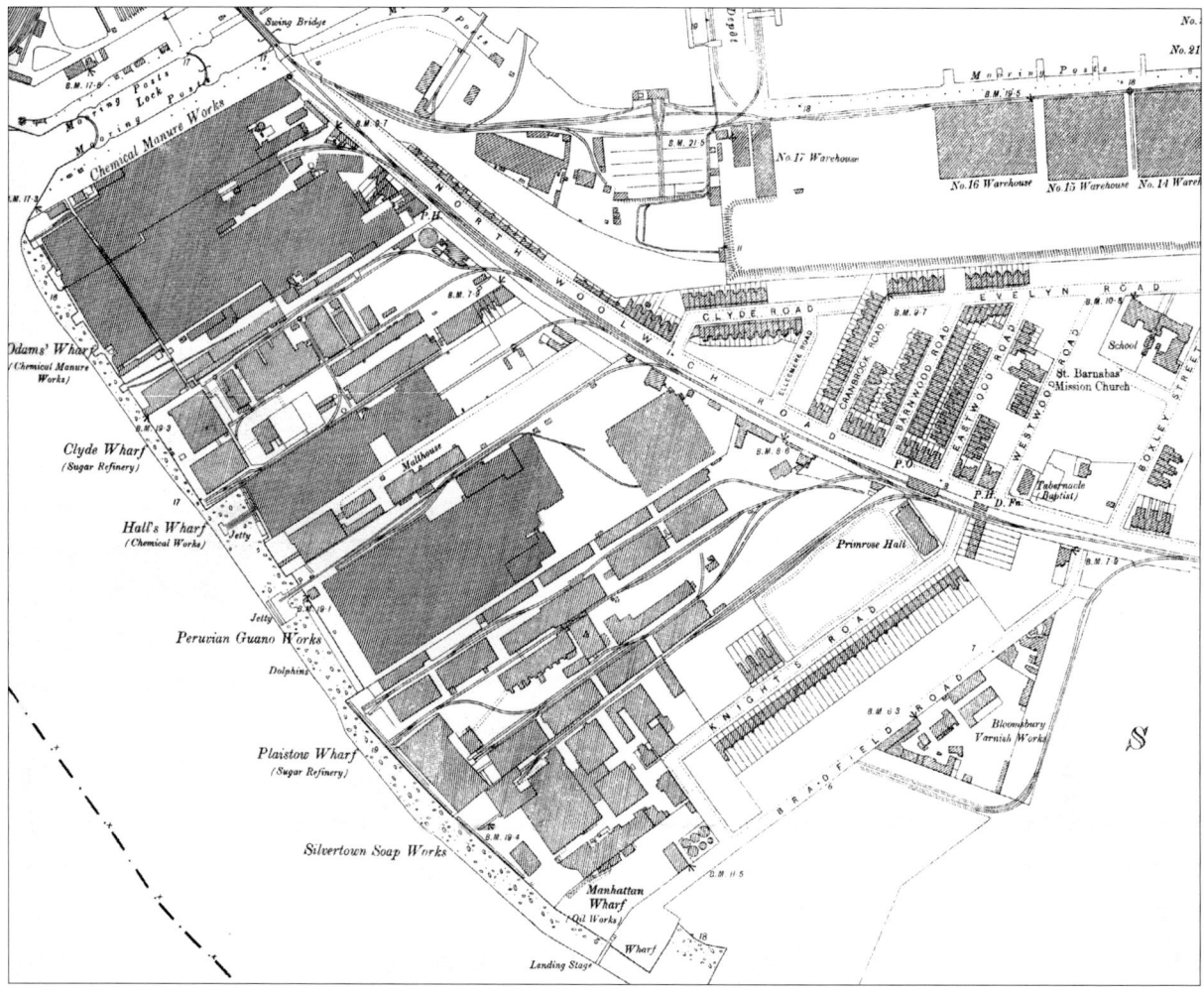

The western end of the Silvertown Tramway near the entrance to Victoria Docks was home to many railway-served industrial premises of chemical factories, sugar refineries and soap works shown on this 1893 map. (Crown Copyright)

The Silvertown Tramway

the cutter's torch. The yard had opened in 1906 and saw countless locomotives pass through, being bought and sold – or scrapped there. Having been taken over by Rio Tinto Zinc in 1982 the scrap business was run down from 1983 and rail traffic there had ceased by 5th September 1991. Amongst the numerous locos resident there the following are of note:

MW	0-4-0ST	No 901/1885	*Harboro*
HC	0-4-0ST	No 1337/1918	*Max*
HL	0-4-0ST	No 2839/1910	*King George*
JF	0-4-0DM	No 4210076/1952	*Thames*
JF	0-4-0DM	No 22934/1941	
RH	4wDM	No 273929/1946	
FH	4wDM	No 3641/1953	
JF	0-4-0DM	No 4210003/1949	
RH	4wDM	No 305314/1951	
FH	4wDM	No 3900/1959	
HC	0-4-0DM	No D1009/1956	
RH	4wDM	No 398611/1957	
HC	0-4-0DH	No D1291/1964	
RR	0-4-0DH	No 10189/1964	
TH	4wDH	No 176v/1966	*Susan*

Following on, there was a large chemical works at Prince Regents Wharf which had been in existence since 1882. The works had both standard and narrow gauge tracks and an early loco there was a 60cm gauge four wheeled petrol mechanical engine No 1738 built by F C Hibberd & Co at Park Royal. This was new in 1931 but was apparently destroyed in a WWII air raid. The site had been taken over by the Prince Regent Tar Company Ltd from 4th July 1934 and, after the war, had been rebuilt by 1947 when a standard gauge fireless loco was purchased new from W G Bagnall & Co of Stafford. This was No 2851 built in 1947 which came under the new ownership of Printar Industries Ltd, a subsidiary of Burt Boulton & Haywood Ltd who took over in 1959. The loco survived until scrapped in November 1969 when the firm closed. The works had been demolished by December 1971.

Tate & Lyle's loco Manning Wardle No 1671 "Elsie" ends its days at the Silvertown scrap yard of Thomas W Ward Ltd. (Robin Waywell Collection)

London's Dock Railways: The Royal Docks, North Woolwich and Silvertown

John Fowler No 4210076 rumbles past T W Ward's offices at Silvertown on 29th July 1970. (Sydney Leleux)

Thomas W Ward's final locomotive at their Silvertown Yard was TH No 176v named "Susan" seen there on 30th July 1989. (Howard Earl photograph/ Copyright Industrial Railway Society)

The Silvertown Tramway

Hudswell Clarke No D1009 stands inside the gate at T W Ward's yard at Silvertown on 26th July 1983. (Ken Scanes)

Another of T W Ward's fleet of locos was HC No D1291 pictured at Silvertown on 3rd December 1985. (Ken Scanes)

Bagnall fireless loco No 2851 seen at the Prince Regent Tar Co Ltd works at Silvertown on 16th March 1957. (Robin Waywell Collection)

Looking westwards along the section of Silvertown Tramway passing the Prince Regent Wharf on 15th August 1962. (A E Bennett/Transport Treasury)

The Silvertown Tramway

The Mineral Oil Corporation was established at Minoco Wharf in 1896 to build a wharf and plant for the importation of oil from Russia. The wharf was later taken over by Gulf Oil in 1929 who, from April 1930, employed a Manning Wardle 0-4-0 saddle tank No 810 built in 1881; nothing further is noted of the loco. The site was latterly run by Silvertown Lubricants Ltd.

At the Crescent Wharf of ICI Ltd there were 10 locos in operation between 1912 and 1961. The chemical works of Brunner Mond & Co Ltd had been established there since around 1881 and, during the First World War, produced TNT. The folly of such manufacture in a built up industrial and urban conurbation became disastrously apparent on 19th January 1917 when a fire at the factory led to the biggest explosion in London's history and destroyed much of the surrounding area. The cause of 73 deaths and 300 more injured was said to be heard as far away as Southampton and Norwich. By 1920 a 2ft 6in gauge railway had been in use there and was operated by four 4-wheel battery electric locomotives supplied new over a period to 1930.

These were:
BEV numbers 194/1920, 393/1922, 622/1925 and WR No 778/1930

ICI had taken over the plant from December 1931 and the narrow gauge locos all eventually went to their Winnington plant in Cheshire. The works closed in March 1961 and standard gauge rail traffic ceased soon afterwards with the site subsequently taken over by Wood & Plastics Ltd. Standard gauge locos used there over the years were as follows:

EB	0-4-0WT	No 10/1880	*Solvay*
RP	0-4-0ST	No 13111/1888	*Walter*
S	4wVBT	No 6893/1927	*Hassall*
S	4wVBT	No 7297/1928	*Wheelock*
RH	4w DM	No 299103/1950	*J B Gandy*
HL	0-4-0ST	No 3721/1928	*Ettrick*
KS	0-4-0WT	No 3048/1917	*Black*
KS	0-4-0WT	No 4199/1920	*Crookes*
MW	0-4-0ST	No 1135/1891	

and an unidentified 0-4-0ST

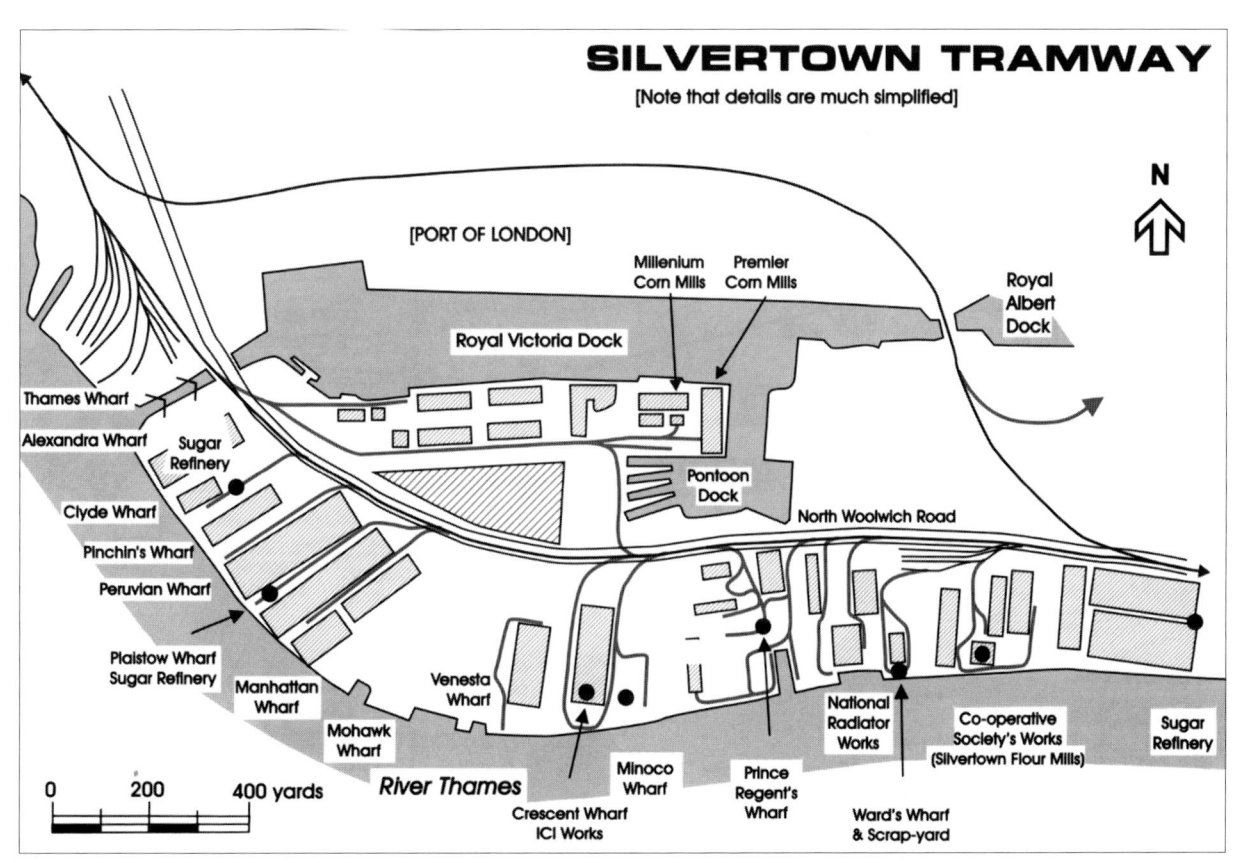

The industrial premises along the tramway in its latter years. (Map by Roger Hateley)

The ICI works at the Crescent Wharf had two Kerr Stewart locomotives. Above is "Black" No 3048 built in 1917 and below is "Crookes", dating from 1920. Both engines came from the company's Winnington Works in Cheshire and remained at Silvertown until the works closed in 1961. (Both Author's Collection)

The Silvertown Tramway

The plywood factory at Venesta Wharf had an internal railway unconnected to the main tramway. The site was destroyed in the Brunner explosion and rebuilt as the Bloomsbury Varnish Works. The oil works at Manhattan Wharf had a railway connection but no locos of its own. The adjacent Royal Primrose Soap Works of John Knight opened in 1880.

Abram Lyle & Sons (later Tate & Lyle) had a sugar refinery at Plaistow Wharf from 1882 and, although no locos are listed there, in 1883 they were advertising for a saddle tank loco capable of hauling 20 tons up a gradient of 1 in 40. Further sidings were connected to the tramway at the Peruvian Wharf where there was a Guano works from 1880, as was the Plaistow Malt Works. Hall's Wharf was the site of yet another chemical factory.

There was also another sugar refinery at Clyde Wharf where the firm of Duncan Bell & Scott was established as far back as 1862. In 1870 a new John Fowler road engine was converted for rail use at the refinery but the works closed in 1886 and it was put up for sale along with twenty one 10-ton railway trucks in 1887. Eventually the business was sold by auction and reopened in 1890, only to be destroyed by fire in 1893. The final connected premises at the western end of the tramway was Odam's Wharf, the site of the Odam Chemical and Manure Company from 1852 which turned out nitrates and phosphates.

Although it continued to be owned by the dock company, and latterly the PLA, operation of the tramway remained under the LNER, then ultimately BR and by 1964 there was still an impressive list of 18 companies with railway connections:

- Standard Telephones & Cables Ltd
- Loders & Nucoline (Cairn Mills)
- Tate & Lyle (Thames Refinery)
- Keiller & Sons (Tay Wharf)
- Co-operative Wholesale Society (Mill Siding)
- Co-operative Wholesale Society (Soap Works Siding)
- Thomas W Ward & Co.
- Spencer, Chapman & Messel (Siding No 1)
- Spencer, Chapman & Messel (Siding No 2)
- Printar Ltd
- Silcocks & Co
- Gulf Oil Co (Minoco Wharf)
- I C I Ltd (Crescent Wharf)
- John Night Ltd (Royal Primrose Soap Works)
- Tate & Lyle (Plaistow Wharf)
- Tate & Lyle (Peruvian Wharf)
- Pinchin Johnson Ltd
- B O C M (Union Works)

Following the decline of the Royal Docks in 1981 traffic on the tramway dwindled and most of the line had fallen into disuse by the mid 1980s. After closure in 1991, much of it was turned into a cycle route and a section now accommodates the Docklands Light Railway on a viaduct above it.

The Silvertown Tramway was nearing its demise and partly dismantled when this photo of BR No 08233 was taken. The loco itself was scrapped in March 1982. (Bert Moody Collection)

London's Dock Railways: The Royal Docks, North Woolwich and Silvertown

Looking eastwards towards Silvertown. A section of the tramway passing through the industrial landscape of 15th August 1962. (A E Bennett/Transport Treasury)

The Silvertown Tramway

The western end of the Silvertown Tramway looking north west from the Thames Wharf area towards Bow Creek on 15th August 1962. (A E Bennett/Transport Treasury)

London's Dock Railways: The Royal Docks, North Woolwich and Silvertown

BR No 08233 crawls over a tramway level crossing on its way to Silvertown and beyond. (Bert Moody Collection)

BR No 08233 hauls a train of empties from the tramway though the rebuilt Silvertown station around 1980. (Bert Moody Collection)

CHAPTER 8

Contractors Railways

The construction of London's docks, and the later repairs and alterations, were in the main carried out by independent contractors who often laid down temporary railways that were operated by their own locomotives to transport heavy materials around the various sites. These were mainly four- or six-wheeled, saddle tank engines. Some of these have been referred to in earlier chapters but it is worth noting them collectively to illustrate the numbers and types used. The major works relevant to this volume were as follows.

Lucas & Aird – Victoria Dock Extension (Albert Dock) 1875–1880

Originally named as the Victoria Dock extension, this became the Royal Albert Dock when completed in 1880. A report of the time states 17 locos were used on the contract and a visit in July 1877 noted 16 in attendance. Nine of these were new Manning Wardle saddle tanks. A serious fire swept through the docks shortly after completion of the works and three damaged locomotives were advertised for sale, one of which was a vertical boilered engine. It is known that both *Chelsea* and *Long Wind* were victims of the blaze but were afterwards used by the dock company on its Royal Albert Dock Passenger Railway (see that chapter). Twelve locomotives are identified as follows:

MW   0-6-0ST No 588/1876 named *Rushton*
MW   0-6-0ST No 589/1876 *Victoria*
MW   0-4-0ST No 606/1876 *Duval*
MW   0-6-0ST No 607/1876
MW   0-6-0ST No 619/1876
MW   0-6-0ST No 621/1876
MW   0-4-0ST No 624/1876
MW   0-4-0ST No 625/1876
MW   0-4-0ST No 631/1876
MW   0-4-0ST No 690/1878
Bton   0-6-0ST No ?/1865 *Chelsea* (see Victoria and Albert Dock chapter)
Long   0-6-0ST built 1847 *Long Wind* (see Victoria and Albert Dock chapter)

London & St Katharine Dock Co – Royal Albert Dock Extension 1884–1886

Works were undertaken by the docks company itself to build a new entrance lock and for the enlargement of the Gallions Basin. Four new locomotives and one second hand were purchased to work along with the company's existing Shanks engine. After completion of the project all were offered for sale by auction on 12th October 1887 but were then retained for dock work.

MW   0-4-0ST   No 893/1884
MW   0-4-0ST   No 905/1884
HE   0-4-0ST   No 343/1884
FE   0-4-0ST   No ?/1884
RP   0-4-0ST   No ?/1870
Shanks 0-4-0ST   No?/1872

S Pearson – Royal Albert Dock Extension 1912–1918

Pearsons were engaged to construct this large extension to the Royal Albert Dock which afterwards was named King George V Dock, being the last of the Royal Docks to be built. Work was carried out on behalf of the Port of London Authority, commencing on the 18th July 1912 but the intervention of the First World War saw the work suspended and the contract surrendered on 2nd August 1918. The PLA, using direct labour and hiring plant and locomotives from Pearson, completed the dock which opened on 8th July 1921. Locomotives employed there were:

MW   0-6-0ST   No 841/1882   *Woolwich*
MW   0-6-0ST   No 858/1882   *Barking*
HE   0-4-0ST   No 420/1887   *Wye*
MW   0-6-0T   No 1196/1890 *Corston*
HE   0-6-0ST   No 550/1892   *Marfleet*
HE   0-4-0ST   No 620/1895   *Joe*
HE   0-6-0ST   No 630/1895   *Canada*
BH   0-6-0ST   No 1105/1895 *The Auditor*
HC   0-4-0ST   No 477/1897   *Willie*
P   0-6-0ST   No 720/1898   *Somerford*
P   0-6-0ST   No 806/1900   *Londonderry*
HE   0-6-0ST   No 717/1900   *Banbury*
HC   0-6-0ST   No 560/1900   *Ladysmith*
P   0-6-0ST   No 939/1902   *Abbey*
P   0-6-0ST   No 958/1902   *Queen*
HC   0-6-0ST   No 833/1910   *Beckton*
P   0-6-0ST   No 1240/1910 *Sir William Crundall*

Sir William Arrol & Co – Royal Albert Drydock 1921

A contract was let to Sir William Arrol & Co for the building of a drydock during works that were underway for the dock itself. The facility was for the use of ship repair firm R & H Green & Silley Weir. This was completed in 1921 with one loco recorded there:
HE   0-6-0ST   No 574/1893   *Trudy*

125

Sir Robert McAlpine – Royal Victoria Dock rebuilding and New Quays 1936–1937

The rebuilding of the Royal Victoria Docks in the mid 1930s. The original finger jetties along the north quays were removed and the new quays at the south east corner of the dock, which had remained undeveloped since its opening in 1855, were developed. The works ran from 1936 to 1937 and two 3ft 0in gauge locomotives were involved:
HC   0-4-0ST No 1535/1924
HC   0-4-0ST No 1536/1924

Edmund Nuttall – Royal Victoria Docks for Co-operative Society 1944

The Co-op had various premises in and around the Royal Docks where Spillers Flour Mills had been damaged by bombing in World War Two. Spillers leased the Co-op's premises on the south side of Victoria Docks until they had new works of their own and it is possible these works were carried out there at the time. Two 2ft 0in gauge locomotives involved in Nuttall's works were:
RH   4wDM No 189952/1938
RH   4wDM No 200782/1941

Work on the Royal Docks extension in progress on 8th June 1914 by contractor S Pearson & Son. Following interruption by the First World War the works were taken over by the PLA and completed by them in 1921. (PLA)

Index

A
acknowledgments iii
Albert dock
    1880 map 2
    aerial view in 1965 77
all company purchases in order of appearance 84–86

B
Bagnall locomotives
    fireless loco No 2851 118
    No 2739 64
Barclay locomotives
    No 1236 28
    No 1237 29
    No 1294 30
    No 1300 30
    No 1301 30
    No 1302 21
bibliography iii
BR No 08233 121, 124

C
Central Station 90
    1894 map 90
Connaught Road Station 89, 90
    map 89
Connaught Tunnel 103, 108–109, 112
    1894 map 106
Contractors
    Edmund Nuttall 126
    Lucas & Aird 125
    S Pearson 125
    Sir Robert McAlpine 126
    Sir William Arrol & Co 125
contractors railways 125–126
Cory Brothers 96
Crossrail 110
Custom House engineering works 3, 42, 49, 67, 74, 76
Custom House Station 88, 97, 101, 107
    1914 map 87

D
Docklands Light Railway 107, 110
Dubs locomotives
    No 1438 7
    No 1439 8
    No 1440 8
    No 1441 9

E
Edmund Nuttall 126

F
Falcon locomotives
    number not known 13, 17
Fox Walker locomotives
    No 149 9
    No 288 10
    No 263 11

G
Gallions Reach coal wharf, map 94
Gallions Station 94–98
    1894 map 92

H
Harland & Wolff Ltd 41, 58, 67
Hudswell Clarke locomotives
    No 1153 32

Hudswell Clarke locomotives (continued)
    No 1154 32
    No 1155 34
    No 1244 34
    No 1245 34
    No 1254 36
    No 1255 36
    No 1323 36
    No 1324 38
    No 1414 38
    No 1415 38
    No 1453 45
    No 1454 45
    No 1455 46
    No 1596 46
    No 1597 46
    No 1598 48
    No 1719 50
    No 1720 50
    No 1748 50
    No D1009 117
    No D1291 117
Hughes locomotives
    number not known 17
Hunslet locomotives
    No 343 16
    No 2414 52
    No 2876 52
    No 2881 54
    No 2891 62
    No 2889 62
    No 3172 62

I
introduction iv

J
John Fowler locomotives
    No 4210076 116

K
Kerr Stewart locomotives
    No 3048 *Black* 120
    Crookes 120
key to manufacturer's names vi
King George V dock,
    aerial view in 1965 77

L
L&NWR locomotives
    No 1819 99
    No 1927 99
    No 1911 100
LB&SCR locomotives
    Chelsea 7
LMS No 4210 59
LNER No 7142 90
locomotive manufacturers, abbreviations vi
locomotives purchased by
    all company purchases in order of appearance 84–86
    London & India Docks Company at Royal Docks 26
    London & India Docks Joint Committee at Royal Docks 23
    London & St Katharine Dock Company 18
    Royal Docks steam locomotives purchased by PLA 71
    Royal Docks diesel locomotives purchased by PLA 83
London & India Docks Company at Royal Docks
    locomotives purchased by 26

London's Dock Railways: The Royal Docks, North Woolwich and Silvertown

London & India Docks Joint Committee at Royal Docks
    locomotives purchased by 23
London & St Katharine Dock Company
    locomotives purchased by 18
London Brighton & South Coast Railway, see LB&SCR
Longridge locomotives
    Long Wind 6
Lucas & Aird 125

M

Manning Wardle locomotives
    No 893 14
    No 905 14
Manor Road Station, see *Manor Way Station*
Manor Way Station 90
    1894 map 91
manufacturer's names, abbreviations vi
Midland Region 3F No 47489 65

N

North Woolwich Railway 101–112
North Woolwich Station 105, 107
    1894 map 105, 107

P

passenger railway
    Royal Albert Dock 87–100
    North Woolwich Railway 101–112
    Silvertown Tramway 113–124
Pearson, S 125
Peckett locomotives
    No 2025 64
PLA
    family tree v
    crest 41
    map iv
Port of London Authority, see PLA

R

Robert Stephenson & Hawthorns locomotives
    No 7103 54
    No 7104 54
    No 7105 56
    No 7107 56
    No 7113 56
Royal Albert Dock extension 1884–1886 125
Royal Albert Dock extension 1912–1918 125
Royal Albert Dock Passenger Railway 87–100
Royal Albert Drydock 1921 125
Royal Docks 27–86
    1880 map 2
    1920 map 40
    aerial view in 1965 77
    diesel locomotives purchased by PLA 83
    pre-WWII railway map 98
    steam locomotives purchased by PLA 71
Royal Victoria Dock rebuilding and new quays 1936–1937 126
Royal Victoria Docks for Co-operative Society 1944 126
Ruston Proctor locomotives
    number not known 15

S

Shanks locomotives
    Victoria 4
    Albert 5
Silvertown Station 103
    1894 map 104

Silvertown Tramway 113–124
    1893 map (western end) 114
    looking west 118
    looking east 122
    looking north west 123
    industrial premises, map 119
    industrial premises 113–121
Sir Robert McAlpine 126
Sir William Arrol & Co 125
Stations
    Custom House 88, 97, 101, 107
    Connaught Road 89, 90
    Central 90
    Manor Way 90
    Gallions 94
    Tidal Basin 102
    Silvertown 103
Stephenson locomotives
    Agenor 22
    No 2844 20
    No 2845 20
    No 2981 20
    No 2982 22
    No 2983 22
    No 3070 24
    No 3050 25
    No 3094 26

T

TH No 176v 116
Tidal Basin Station 102, 106
    1914 map 102

V

Victoria and Albert Docks 3–26
Victoria Dock 1–2
    early map 1
    1880 map 2
    aerial view in 1965 77
Victoria Dock Extension (Albert Dock) 1875–1880 125
Victoria Dock Station, see *Tidal Basin Station*

W

William Cory & Son 9
Woolwich abandoned line 101

Y

Yorkshire locomotives
    No 284 12
    No 2758 80
    No 2759 80
    No 2760 80
    No 2761 80
    No 2762 81
    No 2763 82
    No 2769 82
    No 2770 82
Yorkshire "Janus" locomotives 70
    No 2690 78
    No 2691 78
    No 2739 78
    No 2740 78

London's Dock Railways Part 1
The Isle of Dogs and Tilbury
by Dave Marden

The railways in and around London's docks were arteries to the national railway system at a time when all heavy goods were moved by rail. As well as freight, the Port of London moved vast numbers of people by train around its domain – not just ships' passengers but also dock workers, who were transported from their city dwellings to a host of dockside locations. This book describes the dawn of the major rail-served docks, and traces the evolution of the capital's quayside railways and their locomotives from the days of the early dock companies through to what became the Port of London Authority's huge undertaking.

Over two volumes, we see the growth of the dock company railways from simple sidings to a vast network under the Port of London Authority, together with full histories of over 100 locomotives that worked the various quays and sheds. Part 1 looks at the systems operating in and around the Isle of Dogs at the Millwall and India Docks, and includes various other railway wharves in the area. Also featured is Tilbury Docks which, although remote, were closely associated through company ownership and became part of the PLA network.

The absorbing story of these industrial lines and locomotives is traced from their humble origins to what became one of the largest private railways in the country, but which are now nothing more than a memory that serves to remind us of one of the foremost periods in Britain's industrial history.

Price: £15.95
ISBN: 9781-905505-27-2
120 pages with over 120 photographs and maps

Also available from the same author

Southampton's Quayside Steam

Southampton has long been famous for its docks, but the port also spreads along the banks of the rivers Test and Itchen. Here, lesser wharves have seen their share of rail traffic, and along the whole waterfront, cargoes were moved for over a hundred years by a varied assortment of steam locomotives working behind the scenes.

In this book, Southampton author Dave Marden has compiled a comprehensive record of the steam-operated locations within the docks, wharves and piers of the city's waterfront. Concise histories of each location combine with individual details of the locomotives, following their journeys from various builders' works to their ultimate fates. Also included are details of the many contractors locomotives that have been engaged in the numerous expansions of the docks. The overall result is an extensive and detailed insight into the lesser-known, and certainly less-glamorous, steam engines that have worked along Southampton's quays.

160 pages
Price: £16.95
ISBN: 978-1-905505-02-9

A Further Look at Southampton's Quayside Railways

In this second book about Southampton's industrial and minor railways, Dave Marden has included locations that are slightly further afield, although still within the Southampton area.

The book also features non-steam traction and narrow gauge lines, and while some of the subjects might be a little removed from the more recognisable classes of locomotive, their diversity of design and employment makes them all the more interesting. Some of the lines covered in the previous book have been revisited, particularly those where steam power was superseded by diesel.

The two volumes together present a useful and informative guide to the railways and locomotives that have graced Southampton's waterside – not always attractive but certainly honest and valued workhorses that played such an important role in the city's industrial development and history.

168 pages with over 200 black & white photographs
Price: £17.95
ISBN: 978-1-905505-12-8

The Hidden Railways of Portsmouth and Gosport

This book looks at the lines around Portsmouth Harbour that were operated mainly by the Admiralty and the Military, far from the public gaze. These secretive systems were often obscured by high walls, and most glimpses would have been through closely-guarded gates, with the occasional sight of a train joining the main line. This book brings together data, illustrations and potted histories to give an insight into the locations and operation of these concealed railways.

Of prime importance to Portsmouth is the naval dockyard which was home to over fifty locomotives over the years, but other associated facilities included the Naval Armament Depots at Gosport, the Gunnery School at HMS Excellent on Whale Island and the Army's presence at Hilsea Ordnance Depot – all of which are included.

Several large-scale construction projects also feature, as do railways and locomotives that do not quite fit into the Military or Contractors categories, such as the Stokes Bay Pier and the Lee-on-the-Solent railways. While these were not concealed from the public eye, they are of interest, and are appropriate to the theme of the book. Included for completeness are the dockyard branch lines, the industrial railway at Hilsea Gasworks, and Pounds Yard at Tipner. Although not exactly "hidden", they were beyond public access and fit well into this volume.

160 pages with over 175 photographs
Price: £17.95
ISBN: 978-1-905505-22-7